C.M.BOWRA

ANCIENT

GREEK

LITERATURE

GB30/$1.75

ancient greek
literature

―

C. M. BOWRA

A Galaxy Book

New York   OXFORD UNIVERSITY PRESS   1960

First Published, 1933
First Published as a Galaxy Book, 1960
Second Printing, November 1960

To
RICHARD JENNINGS

CONTENTS

CONTENTS

INTRODUCTION

AMONG European literatures that of ancient Greece has a peculiar place. It is the earliest of which anything has survived, and it has had the widest influence on posterity. The standards, forms, and methods of the Greeks affected the nascent literature of Rome and through Rome the whole culture of the modern world. Even if Greek had no intrinsic or permanent value of its own, it would still be of incalculable importance. But its interest is not primarily historical. Greek literature commands attention because of its intrinsic value, because the Greeks invented and perfected certain types of literary art and produced masterpieces which still excite wonder and delight despite the lapse of generations and vast changes in human outlook. In epic, lyric, and dramatic poetry, in historical, philosophical, and rhetorical prose, the Greeks achieved results so satisfactory in form and so compelling in content that their work has often been held up as a type of perfection and followed as the pattern of what all such work should be.

And yet of this literature, so influential and attractive, we possess only fragments, a mere tithe of what once existed. We have

9

indeed the *Iliad* and the *Odyssey*, the whole of Plato's works, a mass of speeches by Demosthenes, but the reputation of the tragedians is based on the choice of plays set for study in Greek schools, and for Æschylus and Sophocles seven plays each are all that remain of the 80 and 123 which their authors wrote. In other cases the loss is even greater. The epic successors of Homer have left only a few lines, and the brilliant phase of lyric poetry is known largely from tiny excerpts made by grammarians and metricians who cared little for literary merit. Of early tragedy and comedy almost nothing remains, and we have to reconstruct their history from late statements of disputable value. On the other hand, we possess a mass of late literature whose value is small. Useful for the historian and interesting for the student of decadence the works of the grammarians and lexicographers, of the later epic poets and rhetoricians, are a poor substitute for the lost masterpieces of earlier days. The bulk of Greek literature is small and it does not lie outside the powers of a single mind to master its contents, but even within these limits there is much that is almost worthless when judged by standards of literary merit. The deserved reputation of Greek writing depends not on its bulk or its range but on the supreme excellence of some masterpieces which have survived religious fanaticism and the destructive processes of time. These are not numerous, but their style and power place them among the greatest works of man.

For the preservation of Greek literature we are indebted to the learned men of Byzantium, who studied and edited the works they had inherited from the antique world. From Byzantium Greek books came to Western Europe through the indefatigable enthusiasm of the patrons and scholars of the early renaissance, and to these men we owe almost all that we know of the Greeks. In the process of editing and copying some corruption of texts has been inevitable, but on the whole the scribes were conscientious, and we may fairly assume that the texts we now possess are not vastly different from those circulated in antiquity.

This source has in recent years been supplemented by another. Remains of texts written on papyrus have been found in Egypt, and though the bulk of these consists of business documents, among them are remains of pure literature. The lyric poetry which Justinian ordered to be burned was still read in the first centuries A.D., and to Egypt we owe the first book-texts of Sappho, Alcæus and Bacchylides. But this supplement, despite its great interest, is not merely small but lamentably fragmentary. The papyri are mutilated and incomplete. They require the greatest skill for their decipherment, and the numerous gaps in their text can never be filled even by the most skilful scholarship. But their discovery has materially altered our outlook. They have added something to the stock of Greek literature, and they have shown how little we know of what is lost. Greek literature seems to have been richer than its extant remains indicate, and when we pass judgment on it, we must remember that we are dealing with a mere portion of a lost world whose full power and range we are unable to estimate. The remains, no matter how magnificent, are only remains.

The student of modern literature who approaches Greek will be surprised by the ease with which he can accommodate himself to it. Unlike ancient Oriental writings it seems to have been written by men like ourselves. Its great qualities are not fundamentally dissimilar from those we admire in Dante or Shakespeare, and its writers seem to have had a conception of language and its uses which is still generally accepted. Greek poetry achieves its effect through the sustained rhythm of words chosen for their imaginative power, and Greek prose through the persuasiveness and clarity which are essential to eloquence. But with a fuller acquaintance its unique characteristics are revealed, and Greek takes a place as special as that of English or Italian or French. The people and their language show certain constant qualities through their history, and if we can isolate these, we can get some notion of the peculiarities of Greek literature.

INTRODUCTION

Compared with most modern literature Greek is surprisingly simple and unadorned, but this simplicity has nothing in common with the unsophisticated candour of folk-song or the self-conscious simplification familiar among the over-civilized. It is reached through an omission of anything which seems unessential and by an emphasis on what seems structurally or emotionally important. It may be seen in the straightforward art of the epic, in the small scale of tragedy, in the directness of historical narrative. Just as the Greek landscape has a beauty of shape and line, and as Greek sculpture lacks the varied pattern of mediæval or Oriental sculpture in its self-contained and restrained effects, so Greek literature achieves its special distinction by omitting everything that is not essential to the plan of the whole and securing its effect by the power given to each part in its place. The Greeks had a sure instinct for what was really significant, and they omitted everything else. The omission need not have been conscious or deliberate. It was the natural activity of a people whose genius saw where exactly the beautiful lay and how to dispense with preliminaries and elaboration.

This natural artistic sense was allied in the best Greek writers to great intellectual seriousness and power. Seeing many things with unclouded eyes and unbiassed by satiety or prepossession, they brought the full force

13

of their minds to the consideration of their art. They wrote nothing down which had not passed an exacting self-criticism. In particular they avoided the sentimental and the purely decorative. They seem to have felt that poetry must be intimately allied to common experience and be shared with most men. Therefore they built it out of the primary emotions and let alone the twilit corners of sensibility and the fleeting shades of sentiment. They wrote not for cliques but for humanity, and they knew how to distinguish between the temporary and the permanent. Much of their art was popular in the sense that it was performed before large crowds in the open air. But even so they never made the mistake of judging the intelligence of an audience by that of its lowest members. Poetry, being a serious affair, demanded attention and concentration, and the Greek audiences responded to the claims on them, becoming good listeners and intelligent critics. Exposed to such attention the poets had to do their best. There must be no shoddiness and no redundance. Every stroke must tell, every word do its work.

The lessons learned from the study and practice of poetry assisted the Greeks when they came to write prose. Here too we find the same intellectual grasp of essentials, the same economy of structure and freshness of treatment. Greek prose is normally concise and often simple. Truths of great acuteness and situations of real moment are expressed with such directness that at first we are puzzled and feel that it is almost childish. Then we realize that this is another aspect of the Greek desire to state the essential and nothing more. On the whole they disliked fine writing, and for all its subtlety and power their prose seems to avoid anything except its proper purpose of conveying information. But behind the austere exterior lies a reserve of strength. The simplest words may yield a profound truth and an emotion which is all the stronger for being disciplined. Greek prose reaches its effects through the intelligence and touches emotions beyond the reach of superficial rhetoric. Even the orators, who have to appeal to all available emotions, make a strong appeal also to the intelligence. They feel that first they must prove their point.

In consequence of this self-discipline Greek literature lacks many features common in English or Italian, even in Latin. It lacks the vague splendours and the pursuit of the indeterminate which are the life-blood of romanticism. Its epic and its drama seem plain and even prim when placed beside the luxuriant jungle of Ariosto or the teeming life of Shakespeare. The Greek attitude towards nature seems unimaginative until we realize the absolute rightness of every word. Not for them the application of human emotions to stones and trees or the feeling that nature has importance apart from man. In their prose equally we miss many familiar forms. Here are few of the raptures of religious eloquence or æsthetic appreciation, few even of the high austerities of scientific demonstration. There is a lack of the prose epigram and the purple patch. But there is instead an austerity whose concentration and aptness makes much rhetoric look shoddy and much demonstration verbose.

The history of Greek poetry is that of a process in which traditional forms are turned by men of genius into art. Epic, lyric and dramatic poetry all had their origins in simple, perhaps awkward, forms which could not be reckoned seriously as art. But these were transformed by the poets into something quite different, where even the old peculiarities and awkwardnesses contributed to the whole effect. For it is characteristic of the Greeks that they did not invent new forms of literature but perfected those they possessed. To the last their choral odes and their dramas kept the marks of a humble origin. A similar conservatism prevailed in their choice of subjects. In epic, drama and choral lyric their stories were all drawn from the remote past of the Heroic Age, and yet the poet was not only allowed to treat a traditional story as he liked but he was judged by the originality and insight which he brought to it. Like an Italian painter with episodes from the Bible, he could take his story and treat it as he chose, giving it whatever turn or alteration he pleased. In the great treasure-house of myth and saga, the accumulated wealth of youthful fancy and imagination, he could find an almost inexhaustible supply of dramatic and delightful stories. Conscious of having something to say and of his capacity for saying it, he could take a well-tried theme and recreate it, and if he really made something new and good, his success would soon be recognized.

He was of course helped by the peculiar qualities of the Greek language. Its flexible syntax simplified the expression of complicated thought ; its vast vocabulary, formed from many dialects and older obsolete tongues, allowed an almost endless variety of style ; its combination of short and long syllables permitted a peculiarly elastic and musical metric quite beyond the reach of any modern European language. The writer of prose, no less than the poet, employed words whose force and freshness had lost nothing in use and whose evocative power had not been dulled by convention or ineptitude. New compounds could always be invented, new metaphors exploited, new effects made from a small alteration in word-order or a dexterous collocation of vowels. Tradition helped instead of hindering by providing for the poet's use a store of delightful and useful expedients which he could use as and when he liked. Even to-day, when the pronunciation of ancient Greek is a vexed question and the associations of its words are perceived dimly through the mist of years, the language is still bright and luminous, still stamped with the power and directness of the men who used it.

In spite of its restrictions Greek literature is never arid as its imitations have sometimes been. Perhaps it lacks vagueness, fancy, and sentiment, but it has mystery, imagination and passion. The discipline only serves to bring out the rich equipment which went to its making. The imaginative vision which informs all great literature is particularly noticeable in Greek. What a rapt attention had seized, was conveyed to others with a consummate capacity for communication through words. If the Greeks were not really like children, as the Egyptians told Solon that they were, they had at least the child's gift of seeing things with absolute clarity and concentration. Therefore there was no need for them to enhance their feelings with rhetoric or to seek for majesty in obscurity. Their work is often oratorical, often difficult, but they had to address themselves to crowds and they were grappling with many difficulties for the first time. If they ever felt the temptation to write merely for effect, they did not yield to it. Their attention was turned elsewhere, to the great occasions of passionate tension and intellectual effort in the lives of men whose eyes were open and whose wits were alive.

CHAPTER I

HOMER AND HESIOD

THE origins of Greek literature are lost. The Greeks attributed the first flights of song to Orpheus and Linus and Musæus, but even in antiquity nothing of their works was known, and their existence is open to question. For us Greek literature begins with the name of Homer and the two epics of the *Iliad* and the *Odyssey*. Unfortunately, for more than a hundred years such controversy has raged over these two poems that their place in history has been obscured and even their reputation undeservedly affected. Here it must suffice to say that the *Iliad* and the *Odyssey* were composed in the ninth or eighth century B.C., that their style, construction, and temper imply the existence of a single author, that there is no good reason to abandon an ancient and universally accepted tradition that his name was Homer and he came from the Greek coastland of Asia Minor. On the other hand, it is equally certain that Homer did not create epics out of nothing, that his work was the culmination of a long tradition of bardic poetry, that to this tradition he owed his stories, his language, his metre, many of his

19

devices for making his work intelligible and attractive. He may have even embodied fragments of earlier poems, though he probably altered them in the process. Nor is the text, as we possess it, free from interpolations and linguistic changes. But the creative manner of a great poet reveals itself throughout, and the poems must be the work not of a school of poets but of a single man indebted to a rich tradition.

The *Iliad* and the *Odyssey* are heroic epics. They celebrate the great deeds of a generation which has passed from the earth and did what later men could not do. Their values are those of an age which judges everything by the standards of the heroic man who is equally notable in council and in war. These poems are the echo of events which shook the world, and like other heroic poetry they were composed in the aftermath of war and conquest. The conquerors are settling down in their new possessions, and in the growing civilization bards entertain their masters by the recitation of heroic doings. Homer is already far from the war of which he sings, but he has appropriated the standards of the Heroic Age, and he is an authentic bard, trained in rhapsody and recitation. He composed for listeners, not for readers, and his art is the art which grew in the courts of the Greek conquerors and colonists of Ionia.

The Heroic Age of Greece was the mainspring of the epic tradition. It existed in the thirteenth and twelfth centuries B.C., when the confederated Greek tribes tried to establish new kingdoms in Asia Minor and Egypt. From historical documents we know the anxiety they caused to the Pharaohs and the Hittite Kings, but their own poetic imagination crystallized these racial struggles into the story of the Siege of Troy, the rich fortress which guarded the passage from Europe to Asia over the Dardanelles. In the process many facts must have been distorted, but the epic poets kept the memory of efforts and achievements, even of failures, belonging to an age when men were still the sons of gods. To this tradition we owe the *Iliad*. It tells of the siege of Troy, and though its action falls into the last year of the ten years' siege and the actual capture lies outside its scope, it gives the main characters and issues of the Trojan War. Its action takes place mainly on the battlefield or in the camp ; its chief characters are soldiers, and many of its excitements are military. Its broad plan succeeds in giving a picture of the Heroic Age at war, and the details of fighting are written for men who understand war and could take the fine points of a good fight. At a first reading the *Iliad* might seem to be a great picture of heroic warfare, so full is it of single combats and great attacks, so much space is given to the ebb and flow of armies on the battlefield. A hero has his crowded hour and gets wounded only to be succeeded by another hero. In this the *Iliad* resembles other martial epics, but its plot, though complicated, is really based on an original and important theme.

The *Iliad*, as Homer tells us, is the story of the wrath of Achilles. In this son of a sea-goddess, gifted with all that a man can ask, brave, beautiful, eloquent, but doomed to an early death, the Heroic Age found an ideal embodiment of itself. Even in the defects of his nobleness Achilles is the authentic hero. Therefore Homer took him for his story. But the context in which he placed him is not that which old stories had made familiar. In them Achilles must have been pre-eminently the warrior, who lost his friend Patroclus and revenged himself cruelly on his friend's slayer, Hector. The *Iliad* tells a different tale. The theme of " the wrath of Achilles " has been made into a tragic theme in which Achilles is the protagonist. His tragedy is that in spite of his half-divine gifts he makes the wrong use of his opportunities. He quarrels with his liege-lord, Agamemnon, over a captive girl, and right is on his side. But then he refuses to fight and lets his friends suffer loss and defeat. In their humiliation they ask for his help, and Agamemnon makes generous apologies. But Achilles persists in his refusal. He is now definitely in the wrong. He has broken the principle that a man must stand by his fellows in need. Worse follows. Patroclus asks to be allowed to help the defeated Achæans. Achilles lets him go and lends him his own armour. Patroclus is killed by Hector and the armour stripped from his body. Then Achilles takes the field, but his impulse is entirely desire for vengeance on Hector. Half-mad with anger and merciless to anyone who gets in his way he pursues Hector to death and then intends in defiance of all heroic codes to mutilate his body. In the old story the close came with this savage revenge, but Homer leads to a different conclusion. Hector's father, the old man Priam, comes to ransom the body from the slayer. When he sees the old suppliant " kissing the terrible man-slaying hands which had slain many of his sons," Achilles' heart is stirred to pity. He remembers his own father, and all traces of his passion disappear. He gives up the body ; anger is purged in pity. Disaster has played its part, and Achilles is himself again.

This is the central theme of the *Iliad*, but round this Homer has set another story, that of the fall of Troy. And here too he has his ethical intention. Troy is besieged because Paris has abducted Menelaus' wife, Helen. In spite of entreaties from the Trojans he refuses to restore her, and Troy suffers in consequence. On Troy, as on Achilles, lies the curse of an infatuation sent by the gods. It is clear that Troy will fall and its fall will bring unreckonable miseries of death and en-slavement. But because the Trojans too are heroes, they stand by Paris and pay for their loyalty. And in this tragedy, parallel to that of Achilles, Homer is careful to delineate the chief character. Hector is the ideal opponent and antithesis of Achilles. Born of ordinary human parentage he has the qualities which make a man instead of a hero. His very bravery is deliberate and inspired by love of his country. He has moments of doubt, even of fear. A devoted husband and father, the favourite son of his old parents, he is tied with human responsibilities as Achilles never is. Lovable and admirable, he fights magnificently because he must, but he never for long enjoys the sweet delight of battle. Over him too there hangs the shadow of death. The man is pitted against the demi-god, and the man must perish. Hector seems to belong to an age later than that of the great heroes. He lacks their sublime self-confidence and their freedom from common claims. So in spite of his intimate appeal he is not so important as Achilles, but he is an adversary perfectly conceived for him.

These two themes, of Achilles and Troy, are set in a world of living men and women. Tradition must have provided Homer with the names and leading qualities of his characters, and perhaps to it he owed the epithets attached to them, " Agamemnon, king of men," " white-armed Helen," " Priam of the good ashen spear," " Nestor tamer of horses." But just as he took " swift-footed Achilles " and made him into a tragic hero, so Homer turned these creatures of saga into living

beings. His characters fall into two groups
admirably constructed and contrasted. The
Achæan life is that of the camp. Here are
the High King, Agamemnon, impulsive and
passionate, overburdened with responsibilities
but capable of generous and brave actions, old
Nestor, garrulous, wily and delightful, full of
the garnered wisdom of three generations, the
young Diomedes, who has been taught " ever
to be the best and to surpass other men "
and does not shrink from attacking the gods
in battle, Odysseus, the embodiment of sense
and stratagem. In Troy life is different.
Hector has his supporters in the abductor
Paris, who is not without charm and relics of
physical courage, and in the young and chivalrous princes Sarpedon and Glaucus. But here
the real masterpieces are in the old king,
Priam, worn with disasters but courageously
enduring though he knows that the worst is
yet to come, his wife Hecuba, fiercer than
her husband but lacking his real reserves of
courage, the patient and pathetic Andromache, Hector's wife, and the radiant, tragic
and beautiful Helen. She appears seldom,
but we soon know her weariness and solitude,
her hatred for her own beauty and for the
goddess who gave it her. She is a fitting
object for the deadly struggles which centre
round her.

These different themes and characters are
connected in a story of some complexity,
varied with many episodes and often travel-

ling far from Achilles. But they are held together by one thread—the effort which the Achæans make when Achilles refuses to fight and its results, including the return of Achilles to the field. Naturally in such a poem there is much description of fighting, but Homer knows how to keep it lively. He will vary it with those similes which are the ancestors of all similes, short pictures drawn with great brilliance from the poet's own world. The great Ajax in obstinate retreat is like an ass strayed into a field and refusing to be beaten out of it; Paris running to battle is like a barley-fed stallion running to the pasturage of the mares; Apollo destroys the wall of the Achæan camp as a child destroys a sand castle he has built; the light shines on Achilles' head like the fire lit in a beleaguered city for neighbours to see and bring help. The scene too is always changing. From battle we are transported to the walls of Troy where Hector talks to his wife and tries to take up his child, who is frightened by the plumed helmet and only comforted when his father takes it off, or two opponents will stop fighting and tell delightful stories of ancestors who fought with monsters, or we are enchanted with the shield which Hephæstus makes for Achilles, inlaid with delicious pictures of peace and war.

Homer composed for recitation, and his narrative lacks the close cohesion of books written to be read slowly. He has to emphasize the important points and neglect the rest. Therefore his story seems loosely knit. He omits much that might give greater completeness, and once he has finished with an episode he dismisses it summarily, not troubling to tidy the loose threads of narrative. But these apparent carelessnesses are part of his technical skill. They help the rapid movement of his poem, and no epic travels at such a speed or gives such an impression of active and abundant life. The story is always the poet's first consideration and is never a peg for his philosophy. To this rapidity the conventions of style contribute. The stock lines and epithets make attention easier. But the real secret of the speed lies in the movement of the dactylic hexameter, a metre almost impossible in English, and in Homer's capacity for keeping to the point. His imaginative vision sees exactly what happens, and he reports it as an eye-witness in succinct and vivid words. There is no film between him and his characters, no distortion due to their belonging to the past. He is carried on by his story, and he carries us with him.

In achieving such results Homer is helped by his language. It is in a sense artificial. It was never spoken in ordinary life and takes liberties with rules. It is poetical speech, meant for themes more majestic than common life, full of synonyms and alternative forms, with a rich and adventurous vocabulary compounded from many sources. It is the work of many generations of poets, and its power is the greatest tribute to Homer's anonymous predecessors who perfected it. To them he must owe the beautiful recurring epithets, the " rosy-fingered " dawn, the " loudly-resounding " and the " wine-dark " sea, the " ambrosial " night, the " long-shadowing " spear. To them too he must owe some repeated phrases which have an air of great antiquity and seem to belong to a time when common things were dignified with peculiar titles, the " barrier of the teeth," the " holy might " of a man, the " yellow heads of horses." Yet in spite of archaisms this style seems always natural and appropriate. It is invariably lucid, and its richness serves to keep the subject at the proper level of heroic dignity.

For the *Iliad* is consistently heroic and derives its special power from its sense of human achievements. Homer maintains an outlook which is only possible for a man trained in the standards of the Heroic Age. Because true dignity belongs to man and cannot be lessened by comparison, even the gods must suffer. If Homer makes his men like gods, he makes his gods like men. They have moments of majesty, when Zeus nods and shakes Olympus, when Poseidon crosses the sea in three strides, when Apollo descends with the plague " like the night." But their action is not usually on this plane. Their life is like a holiday, the immortal counterpart of the feasting in a King's palace. So by a curious paradox Homer finds in them that element of comedy which he seldom finds in men. The war-god Ares is wounded and screams for pain ; Hera tricks her husband with amorous wiles ; the love-affairs of Zeus are catalogued with mock solemnity. These divine diversions are almost comic relief and belong to pure art. Homer's religion was not puritanical, and he could laugh at the gods. They are relieved from the anxieties of man, but they are also relieved from his moments of strife and splendour. In their world there is no heroism. There is no need to be solemn about them.

True dignity belongs to man, and he is a sufficient subject for poetry. This is the secret of Homer's outlook. He sees man occupied with great undertakings and menaced with an inevitable doom. In this lies the peculiar pathos of Achilles, and in the sense of the brief moment to be caught lies Homer's characteristic sublimity. When the old men " like crickets " discuss Helen and say " It is no matter for indignation that men should fight for such a woman ; she is strangely like the immortal goddesses to look upon," they express Homer's own view. The war may bring unreckonable horrors, but its cause is strangely magnificent. When Hector's wife is full of forebodings, Hector has no soft comfort for her. He says " there will be a day when holy Ilium shall be destroyed, and Priam, and the people of Priam of the good ashen spear."

But perhaps the most intimate passage is where Achilles, half-mad with the death of Patroclus, refuses to spare the life of Priam's young son, Lycaon : " But, friend, you too must die ; why do you lament in this way ? Even Patroclus died, who was a much better man than you. Do you not see what a man I am, beautiful and strong ? I am the son of a noble father, and a goddess was the mother who gave me birth ; but even over me hangs death and powerful doom. There will be a dawn or a sunset or a midday when some man shall take away my life from me in war, shooting me with a spear or with an arrow from the bow-string."

When Homer composed the *Odyssey*, he must have felt that he could not repeat the tragic effects of the *Iliad*. The *Odyssey* is a story of adventure and its roots lie not in heroic lays but in immemorial folk-tales and popular stories. It tells of a man who after many troubles and wanderings comes home to find his wife besieged with suitors and kills them. This ancient theme is built into an epic of rich complexity by the incorporation of other stories equally ancient and by a plot of great ingenuity and human interest. The story is less diffuse than that of the *Iliad* and there is a greater economy in the structure. The main plan is simple and masterly. The first section tells of Odysseus' home in Ithaca ten years after the capture of Troy. The pathetic but not uncalculating Penelope is uncertain and unwilling to decide whether her absent husband is dead or not. There is some comedy in Homer's treatment of her, but there is also pathos and sympathy for her isolation and perplexity. The suitors who invade her home and devour her wealth are a study in vulgarity, far removed from the heroes of the *Iliad*. In them heroic dignity has given place to self-satisfaction and self-seeking. Their admiration of Penelope is adventitious and perfunctory. What they want is her wealth and the position it brings. They have their personalities and separate traits, but they are all alike contemptible, and Homer is careful to keep us from feeling any sympathy for them.

The chief personality of this section is Odysseus' son, Telemachus. He is on the verge of manhood, shy and sensitive, but the shame he feels at the suitors' treatment of his home prompts him to action, and he risks his life in a voyage to find news of his father. In the course of this we meet some old friends from the *Iliad*, and it is plain that the same hand which created Nestor and Helen is still at work. But the real purpose of the voyage is to create our need for Odysseus. His absence is continually remarked, and we are made to feel a great curiosity about him, to ask where he is, and that is why Homer took such pains to make us feel his absence.

The second section concerns Odysseus himself from the fall of Troy to his home-coming.

It is a masterpiece of story-telling and has been the despair of all its imitators. The construction is partly narrative by the poet, partly a recital by Odysseus himself. By this device we start where we left Telemachus but are taken right back to earlier events. Incidentally Odysseus is made more intimate by having to speak for himself. We see the reckless spirit which carries him into desperate straits and the wits which get him out of them. The poet passes no judgment on him, but plainly he finds Odysseus an ideal of manhood, courteous, courageous, princely, ready for any mishap but pursuing steadfastly his determination to get home and see " the smoke leaping up from his dear native shore."

In this section Homer has retold some ancient stories of fabulous monsters and adventures in uncharted seas. Versions of these stories may be found in folk-lore from Polynesia to Scandinavia, and their antiquity is past calculation. The one-eyed monster tricked and blinded by a stranger calling himself " No Man," the winds let out of a bag to carry a ship all over the sea, the ogress " big as a mountain " who eats sailors, the enchantress who transforms men into beasts, the drug which makes them forget their home, the moving islands and colliding rocks, all these may be paralleled outside Greece. They existed before Homer and would have survived if he had never lived. But Homer's peculiar art is to exalt the fancies of folk-lore into poetry. The primitive versions are concerned largely with animals, with the crafty fox and the jumping hare, but Homer applies them to men. Even the man-eating one-eyed ogre, Polyphemus, has some of the clumsy and bestial pathos of an aboriginal savage. His gluttony and drunkenness, his clumsy jokes, his affection for his ram, make him intelligible and not entirely unsympathetic. And the witches Circe and Calypso, the " Hawk " and the " Concealer," despite their magic and their desert islands, are delightfully human in their admiration and affection for Odysseus.

In one or two places the preservation of ancient stories in other countries shows the quality of Homer's art. An Egyptian story of 2000 B.C. tells of a hero who is wrecked and after floating on a log of wood is washed up on an island, where he sleeps long from exhaustion. He wakes to meet a beautiful serpent who gives him royal entertainment and sends him away in a ship loaded with gifts. In outline this resembles Odysseus' adventures in Phæacia, but instead of the serpent we have the enchanting figure of Nausicaa, the King's daughter, who when she is washing clothes on the beach meets the sea-soiled and naked Odysseus and with perfect simplicity and self-possession clothes him and sends him to her parents. From them Odysseus receives boundless hospitality, and Phæacia is a country where everyone is rich and happy. But even in this Never Never Land Homer creates a real world. The King and Queen have their human side, their anxiety to impress the distinguished stranger, their consciousness that they are the only people in the world who count. To them Odysseus tells his adventures, and this stirring tale of endurance is the proper contrast to their idle, agreeable, and sheltered lives.

Another ancient story is that of the hero who crosses the Ocean and calls up the ghosts of the dead. Connected with the name of Gilgamesh it was familiar in Babylonia and Assyria. Homer too takes Odysseus across the Ocean. He digs a trench and fills it with blood, and the ghosts come up to drink, for only so can they regain for a little their lost vitality. In this remote scene Homer provides something more than necromancy. When they have drunk of the blood, the shades speak. Among them is Odysseus' mother who has died in his absence and of whose death he has not heard. He questions her about it, and she answers : " Neither in my halls did the Far-Seeing Shooter of Arrows come on me and kill me with gentle shafts, nor did any disease attack me, such as most often with hateful corruption robs the life from the limbs, but desire for thee and thy ways, glorious Odysseus, and thy gentleness of heart took away my honey-sweet life." Odysseus tries to embrace her but she slips away " like a shadow or a dream." The old theme of a strange adventure is made intimately human and pathetic.

The second section closes with Odysseus' return to Ithaca on the enchanted ship of the Phæacians, and the rest of the poem is concerned with his adventures at home and their culmination in the slaughter of the suitors. Here Homer returns to the manner of the first section. Events are told on a full scale with free play for character and conversation. Odysseus is revealed in turn to his son, his old nurse, his swineherd, his wife and his father. Recognitions delighted the Greeks, and Homer contrives his with ingenuity and variety. More touching than any is the scene where the old dog, Argus, lying in the dung-heap full of ticks, old and neglected, recognizes his master. He wags his tail and droops his ears, but cannot even crawl up to him, and dies after Odysseus has seen him. Through this series of encounters Homer brings Odysseus to his revenge on the suitors. The speed of the narrative increases, and the note of benevolent comedy yields to something more sinister. The old theme of revenge takes command ; there are portents in the sky, and the seer, Theoclymenus, proclaims them : " Ah ! wretched men, what evil is this you suffer ?   In night are your heads wrapped, and your faces, and your knees below, and lamentation is kindled, and your cheeks are wet with tears. The walls drip with blood, and the fair interspaces ; the fore-court is full of ghosts, and full the court also, of ghosts sped to Erebus and the gloom below. The sun is destroyed out of the sky, and an evil mist is spread over all." Methodically and coldly Odysseus proceeds to his revenge. His triumph is due to his bowmanship, and he shoots down the suitors with unerring aim. The details of the killing show that good shooting was appreciated by Homer, but there is also a fierce delight in the punishment of men " who honoured no one among mortal men, either good or bad, who came unto them."

The slaughter done, we might expect the *Odyssey* to come to a close, but the Greeks liked to end in quiet ease and dignity, and the stray threads of the plot had to be gathered together. Therefore the poem continues until Odysseus has buried the suitors and made himself known to his wife and father. All that is natural enough, but more interesting is the scene where the ghosts of the suitors gather beyond the stream of Ocean and talk with the great heroes of the *Iliad*, and especially with the murdered Agamemnon. Here Homer points his moral and unites the *Iliad* to the *Odyssey*. The array of great dead is in strong contrast to the suitors, men of meaner lineage and unheroic behaviour, and we realize that Odysseus and Penelope belong to the nobler company and that this time nobility has triumphed.

Between the *Iliad* and the *Odyssey* there is a

noticeable difference of temper. The *Iliad*
celebrates heroic strength, but the *Odyssey*
celebrates heroic wit and cunning. Much of
Odysseus' triumph is due to his being cleverer
than his adversaries. In his task he is aided
and abetted by Athena, whose tenderness for
him is delightfully unashamed. She admires
him because he has all the qualities she likes
most in herself. She is not above praising
trickery and dishonesty, though her praise is
not without irony. Odysseus triumphs over a
meaner world because he is in every way a
better man than those who try to dispossess
him. But it is hard to feel that in the *Odyssey*
Homer has kept all his old confidence in life.
The high heroic world is menaced by upstarts
who lack the heroic virtues and think they can
reap rich rewards without qualification of
effort. The slaughter of the suitors seems the
last fling of the heroic generation before it went
down to oblivion. And perhaps this note
of despair, implicit and modified though it
is, accounts for the great praise given to
Odysseus' wits. Wits win their greatest renown when other nobler qualities have failed,
and Odysseus comes into his own when
Agamemnon and Achilles are dead. They
perished and Odysseus survived, because he
was cleverer than they were, and therefore
Homer makes him his hero.

An ancient critic compares Homer in the
Odyssey to the setting sun, " whose greatness
remains without violence," and there is truth

in the words.   If we miss the abundant vitality of the *Iliad*, we are recompensed with greater intimacy and fuller detail.   The chief characters are drawn with more fullness than any in the *Iliad* except Hector, and the whole of life on Ithaca is revealed from the swineherd sleeping among his pigs to the maids flirting with the suitors at the palace, from the secret store-room of Penelope to the busy life at the well or the silent cave to which the gods have their own entrance.   In this world where the sea is never out of sight or hearing, where the goats pasture among the rocks and the crops are grown in hollows on the hill-side, Homer places his drama, and from it he fills the interstices of his story.   It is a small world where everyone is known and a stranger is a great event, where the great and the humble speak on equal terms, and the King's father works in the orchard with gloves to keep off the thorns.   All takes place on misty islands on the edge of the Greek world, far from the plains of Troy or the rich palaces of the Peloponnese.   The isolated members of a royal house are almost alone in their exposure to danger and dishonour.   They fight their battles unaided, and their triumph is that of their inherited nobleness.

Even if we allow for many differences between the *Iliad* and the *Odyssey*, the resemblances are more numerous and striking.   In both there is the same generous understanding of humanity, the same pleasure in the good things of life, in eating and drinking, in wealth and courtesy and hospitality, in skill at shooting or ship-building, in the numerous details of pastoral life, in cows, sheep and pigs, finally in all the natural sights of the Greek world, in the sea-birds diving or perching on rafters, in the rise and fall of the wind, in the return of evening and morning, in the sun and the sea and the sky. If Homer was blind, and the tradition is but poorly founded, he remembered well what he once saw. Few poets have the gift of conveying visible things so clearly as he can. In the *Odyssey* he gives freer play to this gift than in the *Iliad* and writes of harbours safe behind cliffs, of gardens where fruit never fails and caves clothed with creeping vines. He had good ears too, and his verse repeats the scudding of water under a ship, the bleat of ewes in their stalls, the wash of waves on rocks, the bumping of a stone downhill.

But all this is only the background for his great characters. Out of their actions he made his poetry, and though he was capable of lyrical sweetness, he kept to his special art and made the chief interest of his epics what is done and the people who do it. His great effects are of emotion expressed in action, and he secures his object through his characters without ever obtruding his own judgments on life or on them. So in the end he remains impersonal. We know his tastes, what men he liked, what he noticed in the world, but of what he thought, what judgments he passed, what he hoped or feared for his time or his art, he says not a word. The first poet of Europe keeps company with Shakespeare in that his works have been denied to him because he excluded his own name and opinions from publicity and fame. But as a poet we know him. He laid the foundations of Greek literature, and the Greeks turned to him continually for inspiration and example. He was the father of both comedy and tragedy, and though his epic manner could never be successfully reproduced, other poets learned from it how to shape their material and to manage their language. From him too they learned that economy in presenting experience which keeps us wondering that so much can be said in so few words. What he almost alone possesses, what none of his successors in epic has shared, is his wide range of creation. His world was circumscribed by the knowledge of his age, but he packed it with living men and women and fashioned from saga and folk-story characters and events as vivid to-day as when he brought them into existence.

Behind Homer stands a society conscious of success and anxious to hear itself praised, but life in early Greece was not always passed in this noble air. The other side of the picture may be seen in Hesiod whom antiquity claimed to be a contemporary of Homer and whose *Works and Days* may go back to the eighth or ninth century B.C. Hesiod came from Ionia to the mainland and lived in Bœotia where conditions were harder and the glorious past more remote. He belonged to the class of small farmers and thought little of the nobles for whom Homer composed. For him kings are not " sons of Zeus " but " devourers of the people " and his chief interest is in the daily struggle for existence. The *Works and Days* was written for use. It is a handbook for Hesiod's brother, Perses, who is a bad manager and needs advice about farming. It is written by a man who knows what he is talking about, who knows how hard is the struggle for existence but faces the facts courageously and prudently. The poem describes the Farmer's Year in Bœotia in its natural setting, its stories, and its hopelessness.

To this didactic task Hesiod brought considerable qualities. He suffers from the inevitable comparisons made between him and Homer. He had few of Homer's gifts, and he was attempting something new in his application of the epic manner to a didactic subject. The *Works and Days* lacks design and is full of delightful irrelevances. The movement of Hesiod's verse is slower than Homer's, though it has its own dignity and solemnity. But Hesiod is no mean poet. He is the first European poet who writes of nature for its own sake. He knows it with the eye of the farmer who watches every sign and marks its significance. When the crane flies south, he must get in the harvest ; when the cuckoo sings in the oak-leaves, he must put his hand to the plough. He has seen the woods groaning when the winds blow from Thrace and the animals shiver and droop their tails, and he knows those summer days when the cicada sings unceasingly and the goats are fat and the wine is at its best. He knows too that calm at sea when the alighting gull leaves a mark on the water. For himself he prefers the land, but there is money to be made by sea, and he must not hide the fact from a starving world.

This farmer's wisdom is mixed with some delightful stories. Hesiod is the first to tell of Pandora's jar and the Five Ages of Man. His art is lively and skilful. He knows how to make his effect, whether it be the golden necklace which the Graces and Persuasion give to Pandora, or the deaths of the men of the Golden Age " as if overcome with sleep," or the heroes who dwell " in the Islands of the Blessed by deep-eddying Ocean." He has an eye for the significant detail, and though he is unashamedly didactic, he knows how to make even morality interesting. He is a great collector of maxims, and all have the concision and gaiety of the best proverbs. He knows that " potter quarrels with potter, and builder with builder," that " half is more than the whole," and he has wise words to say about a sense of honour which does no good to a man in need and about politeness to neighbours and letting enemies alone. His morality

is entirely practical, but at times he is stirred
to a fine indignation by the presence of injustice in the world, and he denounces princes
who abuse their power. Might may seem to
triumph in nature, and the hawk refuses
mercy to the nightingale in its clutches, but
Hesiod knows that Zeus has his three thousand
immortal guards who watch over men and will
certainly punish those who use crooked justice.

Hesiod was one of a school of poets, and
other works in his manner were attached to
his name. The *Theogony*, written by an
anonymous poet, who refers to Hesiod as his
master, is an exposition of the gods of Greece,
their descent and functions. Apart from its
unrivalled interest for the study of early
religion it has merits of its own. The poet
announces in an impressive exordium that the
Muses have appeared to him, and bade him
tell the truth and inspired him with power to
speak " of things that were before and are to
be." We are introduced to the Olympic gods
and their forerunners, Chaos, Earth, and
Heaven, the Titans and the Giants. In the
unravelling of this complicated piece of divine
history the poet sometimes gets lost in his
anxiety to present his facts correctly, and
poetry yields to exposition. But he has his
great moments, and when he describes Zeus'
conquest of the Titans, he achieves a real
sublimity whose excellence may best be seen
if we compare it even with such masterpieces
of cosmic narrative as the early Norse

43

poems : " No longer did Zeus withhold his strength, but straightway his heart was filled with anger, and he showed forth all his power. Together from the sky and from Olympus he lightened continuously as he walked. His bolts flew with thunder and lightning thick and fast from his strong hand whirling a holy fire. And the life-bearing earth was burned and crackled, and the limitless forest roared loudly with the fire. All the land boiled and the streams of Ocean and the unharvested sea." This is grimmer and simpler than anything in Homer, and it belongs to a more primitive world, but the poet's art is equal to his vision, and that is no small claim.

Hesiod's literary progeny seems to have been prolific. The poetry that followed him seems to have become more instructive and less literary. It exulted in catalogues of names with small descriptions attached, and later its writers were much used as sources for stories or plays. But of this literature very little survives. One complete poem, *The Shield of Heracles*, deserves a mention. It is a description of a work of art and may owe something to Homer's account of the shield of Achilles. But it is an honest piece of writing. Its author is more than a connoisseur of metal-work. He has some sympathy with heroic doings, and he has watched nature with care, noting the wild boar whetting his teeth and foaming at the mouth before he attacks his hunters or vultures fighting over the body of a goat or hind which a man has killed unwittingly and left to die.

While the Hesiodic school were exploiting their traditional folk-lore, the epic poets were busy in Ionia. Homer was followed by a school of poets who filled the gaps between the *Iliad* and the *Odyssey* and completed a cycle of epic poetry from Zeus' decision to reduce the earth's population to the death of Telemachus. Of this vast literature hardly anything survives, though some stray quotations show that it must have been worth reading. But we still possess the remnants of a delightful form closely connected with it. The so-called *Homeric Hymns* were written by bards for recital before the more serious recital of the epic poems at feasts and public holidays. They concern a god or goddess, presumably that one whose feast is being held, and they tell a relevant episode. Some thirty survive, and they vary in length from over four hundred lines to only six or four. Their dates are as varied as their contents, and the latest may come from the classical age. But they have a unity of manner which shows how strong a force was tradition in moulding Greek literature. Their style, based on Homer, is less restrained than his, and sometimes they lack clarity. But the words have the same freshness and the metre the same rapidity. They are authentic products of a great narrative tradition.

The *Homeric Hymns* are never so serious as

the *Iliad*, and they do not treat of stern subjects like Odysseus' revenge on the suitors. They tell of the gods, who being exempt from death and pain live a life that men would like to live but may not. So they are full of humour and joy. They take us into a world of gay adventure, where Hermes tricks Apollo and steals his oxen, where Dionysus is captured by pirates but turns himself into a lion and frightens his captors into the sea, where Aphrodite appears to Anchises on Mount Ida in raiment brighter than the glitter of fire and makes him fall in love with her. Or they take us to a still rarer world where Apollo conducts the heavenly choir, the Muses sing to his accompaniment and the Hours and the Graces dance with their hands on each other's wrists. Nor is at least one poet afraid to make the gods more significant by making them more like men. The *Hymn to Demeter* tells the beautiful story of the rape of Persephone and of her mother's long search for her. The poet has a fine range, from the splendid and terrible scene where Persephone stretches her hand to pluck the magic flower, on which all earth and the sea have smiled, to the pathetic and wistful lines where Demeter, disguised as an old woman, becomes a nurse and is caught by a mother warming her child at the fire to make it immortal. Even the small hymns of a few lines are full of charm, calling up the swan which sings of Apollo, or Earth, or the Hearth, or some other delightful moment in a religion whose festivals were really feasts. The writers of the *Homeric Hymns* were not concerned with the troubles which beset Hesiod or with the great events of which Homer sang. They sang instead of the immortal gods and of the blissful life which was theirs.

CHAPTER II

EARLY ELEGIAC AND LYRIC POETRY

THE conditions which produced epic poetry could not last for ever, and when the age of heroic monarchies gave way to that of more leisured and less militant aristocracies, there was a corresponding change in literature. Personal emotions and experiences took the place of old stories ; amateurs wrote poetry as well as professionals ; poetry itself became more immediate and intimate. The change first becomes evident with the appearance of the elegiac couplet, a variation of the epic hexameter in the direction of lyric verse, which was to endure from the seventh century B.C. to the late products of Byzantium. By combining the dactylic hexameter with alternate pentameters something new was given to poetry. The unit was no longer the paragraph but the couplet, and with the change the poet could express himself in a smaller compass instead of in the unrestricted periods of the epic style. In its first appearances the elegiac couplet lies half-way between the free epic style and lyric monody. It keeps the epic language and rhythm, but the poet talks about himself when he chooses.

The elegiac seems to owe its name and existence to Anatolia. It was originally a song accompanied by flute-playing, and as the flute was used especially for marching and feasting, the first elegiacs are military and amorous. Perhaps the earliest example is a poem by Callinus of Ephesus (fl. 660 B.C.), urging his countrymen to take arms against some unspecified enemy. To judge by the few lines left Callinus had a fine bright style. His appeal is to the sense of honour; since a man must die when he must, why not gloriously in battle instead of living unhonoured and dying unmourned at home? The brave man is the peer of demi-gods; "for as a tower men see him before their eyes, for though he is but one he does deeds worthy of many." More of the same style can be seen in the remains of Tyrtæus (fl. 650–630 B.C.), said to have been an Athenian schoolmaster who came to Sparta and helped by his songs and leadership in the subjection of the rebellious Messenians. He is less of a stylist than Callinus, and his verse is sometimes rough. But he has a fine indignation and a real sense of the horrors of war, as well as of its glories. His appeal is to courage, his call to the young men not to let the old suffer or to spend their own years in beggary or exile. His verse is simple, but it has sincerity and directness and the persuasive power that comes from a direct appeal to pride and prowess.

More talented than either Callinus or Tyrtæus was Mimnermus of Colophon (fl. 630

B.C.). He developed the other side of the elegy, its amatory character. He is the first hedonist of literature, the first poet to proclaim unashamedly that in our short passage to the grave all that matters is pleasure and especially love. Hating old age and death he writes of them with great feeling, and his hedonism is justified by his sense of the fleeting character of all enjoyment. By him the black Fates stand, the one with the doom of painful old age, the other with the doom of death. Man's life passes like the flowers of the spring, and he must enjoy himself while he can; "What life is there, what pleasure, without golden Aphrodite? May I die when I care no more for these things, for secret tenderness and honey-sweet gifts and sleep?" These sentiments are expressed in a style of singular flexibility and sweetness. Mimnermus understood his craft well and borrowed from Homer just as much as he needed. The bulk of his work seems to have been written to a flute-girl, Nanno, and through his Roman imitators, Propertius and Ovid, he is a founder of love-poetry. But he could write equally well on other topics, and a beautiful fragment shows how well he could tell a piece of mythology. He writes of the laborious sun, who has never any respite from his work; for even when he has reached the West, he must travel back under the earth in a golden cup to the Æthiopian land where his chariot and horses are waiting for the Dawn.

The climax of this personal poetry was reached in a man of very different character. Archilochus of Paros (fl. 648 B.C.) was known to posterity as the Scorpion, and his violent, passionate, and attractive personality still breathes through the broken relics of his work. Poor and unsuccessful, he lived an adventurer's life round the Ægean, fighting in Thasos, fighting in Eubœa, unhappy in his love as in his business, quarrelling with his friends and persecuted by his enemies. His masterful intelligence brought him no good except in his art, but in this he seems to have been an original genius who left a lasting impress on the language. If not the inventor, he was at any rate the perfecter of those iambic and trochaic metres which later played such a part in Attic drama. A writer of beautiful elegiacs, he extended their scope to include any theme that suited his whim from the spear which was his food and drink to the shield which he lost in battle against the Thracians. He broke the shackles of Homeric imitation and invented a brilliant dashing style full of colloquial phrases, proverbs, and bold inventions of his own. He followed his emotions and was concerned only with them, and his appalling sincerity is stamped on every word he wrote. He was capable of wishing every evil to his enemies, and he is the first known poet of hate. But he has more tender gifts. In words of delicate simplicity he describes a young girl carrying myrtle and roses, or he foretells the unnatural horrors portended by an eclipse, or he watches the rough sea and waits for the coming storm. He wrote fables about animals, full of wordly wisdom and wit, full too of his own distaste for life. The Greeks classed him as an innovator equal to Homer, and it is sad that we cannot enjoy the full range of his genius.

While personal poetry grew in Ionia and the islands, the mainland matured its traditional forms in a different manner. From the beginnings of their history the Greeks had had songs accompanied by music and dancing. These might be in honour of a god or goddess or belong to some specially holy season or place. They were largely concerned with the great occasions of birth and marriage and death, with vintage and harvest, with pestilence and famine. The song was sung by a choir which performed rhythmical movements and was directed by a leader. Homer records such singing, but simpler forms might be seen in children's games whose memory is preserved. For instance, one party of children would sing

" Where are my roses, where are my pansies, where
    is my beautiful parsley ? "

and the other party would answer

" Here are your roses, here are your pansies, here
    is your beautiful parsley."

There were many such games, and at Sparta they were part of education and sung by organized choirs. All children were trained in them, and the transition was not difficult from this simple form to an elaborate art.

From such songs and dances grew Greek choral poetry, a form of art deeply associated with ceremonies and requiring of its makers a knowledge of music and dancing as well as of verse. Throughout its history it kept features implicit in its origins. Nearly always it told of some god or hero, perhaps because it was connected with his festival. It was a great repository of moral maxims. Unlike Homer, the choral poets felt called to make statements about life and behaviour, and from all comes the same message that man must remember his mortal state and not try to rival the gods. It also contained personalities. The poet could speak freely about himself or the members of his choir. He could praise a patron or a host, and this often led him to tell episodes of family history. These heterogeneous· elements make choral poetry difficult to understand, and sometimes its allusions seem irretrievably lost. Indeed, of all the forms of Greek poetry it is perhaps the most remote from modern taste. But for the Greeks themselves it was bound up with the most solemn and glorious occasions in their lives, and to it they confided some of their most intimate thoughts. Though at times it seems stiff and formal and though it is never easy to follow, this choral poetry has moments of concentrated magnificence and real sublimity.

In the more popular art of the epic these special beauties are not to be found, and by its possession of them the choral ode takes us to the heart of Greek life.

At Sparta in the seventh century B.C. the authorities patronized the arts and imported musicians and poets. A Spartan literature began with Terpander (fl. 676 B.C.), who wrote hymns, and Tyrtæus, who wrote elegies. Spartan festivals already included choral dances for girls and boys, and the new poets wrote for the old needs. The measure of their success may be seen in a beautiful, difficult and mutilated poem written by Alcman (fl. 630 B.C.) for a choir of maidens. Alcman came from Sardis in Lydia, but he assimilated the Spartan dialect and Spartan ways. In the Maiden Song he shows the traditional features of the ode—the myth, the maxims, and the personalities. Indeed, the last are so intimate that they are far from clear, and the intention of the poem is still uncertain. It seems to have been sung before dawn at some religious festival. Other choirs are competing, but Alcman's choir hopes for the prize because of the beauty and talents of its leader, Hagesichora, who may not sing as well as the Sirens— for they are divine—but is at least like a swan on the River Xanthus. Despite its lost allusions the poem is full of brilliant images and melodic beauty. The delicacy which compares the girls to colts or birds, the short nervous sentences, the swift movement of the metre, give delightful glimpses into an all but lost world.

Other fragments of Alcman show that he was capable of writing with crystalline limpidity. Two deserve quotation. In one, written when he was old, he regrets that he can no longer take part in the dance : " No longer, maidens with honey-sweet tones and voices of desire, can my limbs carry me. Would, ah ! would that I were a kingfisher, who flies with the halcyons over the flower of the wave, having a careless heart, the sea-blue bird of the spring." In the other he describes night : " The peaks and the valleys of the mountains are asleep, the promontories and the water-courses, and all the tribes of creeping things which the black earth nurses, wild beasts who roam the mountains and the family of bees, monsters in the depths of the blue sea, and the tribes of the long-winged birds are asleep." The cry that the Greeks had no poetry of nature is disproved by this.

Alcman is the only choral poet of the seventh century from whom any words survive. His contemporaries in Ionia were writing neat and bitter satires, preferably on women. There is not much merit in Simonides' (fl. 630 B.C.) equation of different sorts of women with different animals, nor does his imitator Hipponax (fl. 542 B.C.), who revived his art in the next century, indicate that much has been lost with their works. But about 600 B.C. the island of Lesbos gave a new poetry to the world. The poetry of Sappho and Alcæus may perhaps have its origins in folk-song, but it is neither choral nor popular. It was written to be sung before their friends; its origins are local and personal. But because of the genius of its writers these boundaries are transcended, and the appeal of this poetry is universal. In Sappho and Alcæus sensibility and passion were perfectly united to consummate craftsmanship. They had much of the greatest importance to say, and they knew exactly how to say it. Sappho's language has the simplicity of plain speech raised to the highest pitch of expressiveness. She uses hardly a word that does not belong to her vernacular, but her choice is faultless and her arrangement inevitably right. She has the art of metre at her finger-tips. Each stanza is the perfect vehicle for the emotion it conveys, and the words fall into it without any stress or effort. She is an exponent of the highest style in which nothing can be other than what it is.

Sappho lived with a circle of women and girls between whom there was little formality and no artificiality. To these friends her poems are addressed, and as she felt powerfully and deeply, her work has often the power of tense passion. Her name, maligned by the corrupting imaginations of Alexandria and Rome, has suffered from her passionate attachments and unrestrained tenderness, but no one who reads her poetry can feel that it is the reflection of anything but the purest love. She is the perfect exponent of the pangs of unrequited passion, of the regret of parting and the memory of old love. These eternal topics are treated by her with a directness that makes metaphor otiose. She states the facts with such power that they are sufficient in themselves, and the smallest fragments of her work are still instinct with life. She has only to say " I loved you, Atthis, once—a long time ago " or " the spring's messenger, the love-voiced nightingale " or " I have a lovely child with beauty like golden flowers, Cleïs, my beloved," and nothing can be added or taken away.

Her longer pieces tell of the intenser moments in her emotional life. She prays to Aphrodite to keep her promise and release her from the anxieties of love, or she tells how in the presence of her beloved her lips are sealed, her eyes blind, and her ears full of a buzzing. Or she writes of a friend who has gone to Lydia and " surpasses the Lydian women as when the sun is set the rosy-fingered moon surpasses all the stars. The dew is spread abroad in beauty, the rose blooms, the tender grass and the flowering clover." Or in simple, direct words she writes of a friend who has broken her promise to remember her and the happiness they once shared. But she does not always write under the strongest stress of passion. She is capable too of pure joy, when she hears the water pattering among the apple-trees or sees the moon swelling to fullness or the evening-star bring back the sheep and the goat and the child to its mother. She can write with scorn of an ignorant woman who will flit dimly among the unsubstantial ghosts because she has never plucked from the Pierian rose-tree, or with exquisite and fitting beauty of a young bride,

Like the sweet apple which reddens upon the top-
    most bough,
A-top of the topmost twig,—which the pluckers
    forgot, somehow—
Forgot it not, nay, but got it not, for none could get
    it till now.[1]

Song came naturally to her unimpaired sensibility, but her powers were more than those of mere song. She touched with complete mastery on the strongest passions and turned them to music. She assailed the hardest tasks of poetry and she succeeded, as only the very greatest have succeeded, in saying in perfect words what she felt in her moments of concentrated insight and un-imaginable excitement.

Her friend, Alcæus, had not her intensity nor her feminine susceptibility. He was a man of action, concerned with war and pleasure, and his poetry is the record of his busy life. He resembles those cavalier poets who wrote songs in the intervals of fighting, but his power is stronger than theirs. He is essentially mascu-line, and his verses have a toughness and force

[1] Trs. D. G. Rossetti.

that accord with his soldierly character. Less
adventurous in his metres than Sappho and
less a master of the vernacular, he was still
a considerable craftsman, capable of conveying gay intoxication or bitter hatred or
religious devotion as his mood dictated. His
most famous poems were concerned with his
long fight against the Lesbian tyrants, Pit-
tacus and Myrtilus. Against them he gave
full play to his spleen, and he was a master of
abuse. He invented the famous figure of the
ship of state and wrote bravely and nobly of
the perils in front of himself and his friends.
He wrote too with great charm of his own life,
welcoming his brother back from Babylon,
where he had slain a man five cubits high, or
praising " violet-haired, holy, sweetly-smiling
Sappho." His hymns seem to have been full
of grace ; he had an eye for the picturesque
detail, for Peleus bringing the Nereid, Thetis,
to be his bride in the centaur's cave, or for
Castor and Polydeuces, the divine brothers
who appear as lights in the storm and save
ships from wreck.

After Sappho and Alcæus there was no more
poetry in Lesbos, but further south Anacreon
(c. 563–478 B.C.) inherited the art of personal
monody. Time has been unkind to Anacreon.
His innumerable imitators have soiled his
name and made him a type of bibulous and
lecherous senility. His genuine fragments do
not confirm this impression. Compared with
his imitators Anacreon is remarkably healthy.

He enjoyed his life and complained when the end drew near. He was unashamedly fickle; he liked drinking; his passions were neither lasting nor profound. But he is an excellent poet of pleasure. He gaily took what came, and wrote with a style that is at once light and strong. Even when the prospect of death appalled him, he wrote of it half in mockery. He saw himself with hoary temples and decaying teeth, and he did not like the grim pit of Tartarus; but he laughed at it while he wrote of it, and no doubt he died as gracefully as he had lived. He judged life by the pleasure it gave him, but he kept his wits lively. His imitators at Alexandria and Byzantium have left a large number of poems modelled on his which had an enormous influence on the literature of the Renaissance in France and England. But despite their charm they do not approach the original. Anacreon was a poet of pleasure, but he was also a master of words and a highly intelligent man.

Anacreon's world is very unlike Alcman's. The sixth century was a time of expansion and change. The ordered life of the self-contained Greek cities was affected by new political movements and freer interchange of experience. Anacreon himself did not write for his friends at home, as Sappho and Alcæus had, but found patrons where he could and lived under princely patronage in Samos, at Athens, and in Thessaly. The poet's profession had become migratory. He must move on when his patron died or grew tired of him. The result was that poetry, especially choral poetry, lost its roots in local cults and rites, and the poets developed an almost international manner, writing a composite language made of different dialects and using the common stories of the Greek world instead of local traditions. In the course of winning their bread they had also to subordinate their personalities to the whims of their patrons and even at times to express sentiments which they did not fully share. On the other hand, the necessities of competition and the desire to please made them exert their powers to find new variations in their art, and the sixth century carried the choral ode to its maturity.

The great figure in this change was Stesichorus of Himera (*c.* 630–553 B.C.) whose importance can only be gauged by what the Greeks say of him, as his scanty fragments give little idea of his powers. He seems to have uprooted the choral ode from its ritual connections and turned it into a form of lyrical narrative. He extended its length and scope, altered its structure and devised new metrical effects. He was extremely enterprising in his choice of subjects. He helped or started the career of famous themes such as the murder of Agamemnon or the Egyptian Helen. His influence was enormous on Pindar, in whom we can see the enrichment given to the choral ode by this enterprising choir-master. Another Greek from South Italy, Ibycus of Rhegium (fl. 560 B.C.), shows both the advantages and the defects of the changed conditions. He had a great name as a poet of love, and two fragments show a passionate sweep that for all the gorgeous trappings recalls Sappho. In one he writes of a garden in the spring, with apples and streams and vines, but on him Love blows like a north wind and shakes him from head to foot. In the other he finds himself being driven into Love's boundless net and he trembles like an old chariot-horse going unwillingly to the race. In these two poems Ibycus has a real affinity with the Elizabethan song-writers and his sincerity is beyond question. But he had also to write for a living, and a new fragment from Egypt shows him as the adroit courtier of the tyrant of Samos and his son. This is court poetry meant to please and amuse, and if the poet's heart is not in it, we must not complain.

While choral poetry developed in this way, the elegiac continued to be the vehicle of leisured men writing for their own satisfaction. The Athenian law-giver, Solon (fl. 594 B.C.), used it for his political opinions and philosophy of life. He is not a great poet, but he has homely virtues of honesty and good sense, and he has too a seriousness and dignity which give power to his statements about politics. Athens lay near to his heart and what he says of it is noble and generous. But his verses are insignificant in quantity and quality when compared with the considerable collection attached to the name of Theognis (fl. 520 B.C.). If all these poems were by Theognis, we should have a full knowledge of the elegiac in the sixth century and a poet's works well preserved instead of in shreds and patches. But the collection is more probably an anthology from different poets between about 700 B.C. and 460 B.C. A genuine Theognis may be strained out of this medley, and he is a poet of first-rate interest. A Megarian aristocrat, deprived of his estates and driven into exile, he shows to the full the ideals and temperament of the landowners who were disappearing before the triumph of democracy.

Theognis' poems are mostly addressed to his squire, Cyrnus, and expound his soldierly and chivalrous outlook. For him the nobles are the good and the people the base. With the first we should associate, but the second destroys the wits. His aristocratic ideal has its foundations in a creed. He believes in the breeding of men as of rams and asses ; he has a nobleman's conception of pleasure. He likes wine and hospitality and the company of his equals. He is a type, familiar enough in history, of the exiled landowner complaining of injustice and abusing his expropriators. But he raises his complaints to the level of poetry. He has an excellent eye for an apt image ; he can clinch an epigram in a dexterous couplet. He can be genuinely touching when he hears the bird's cry proclaiming spring and his heart is fluttered because other men own his fields. His best poem is his promise of immortality to Cyrnus. The majestic march of the lines through the promise of immortal glory on the lips of men concludes with a pathetic and painful couplet in which he complains that Cyrnus mocks and tricks, and the surprising close recalls some of Shakespeare's Sonnets.

With Theognis the age of personal poetry has almost passed. In Athens at the end of the sixth century delightful songs, usually political, were sung at banquets in honour of popular heroes or clinching a piece of proverbial wisdom. But the great figures of the age were Simonides (556-467 B.C.) and Pindar (522-448 B.C.). Both were exponents of the choral ode and both professional writers who toured Greece. Both had a high sense of their calling, and though their personalities were opposed and even antipathetic, their success was the same. They showed what could be made of the choral ode by a master, and with them it reached its supreme phase.

Simonides was honoured as a wise man. His words were quoted as examples of ripe judgment, and in his fragments there is a predominantly ethical note. The longest is a severe sermon to the King of Thessaly on pride. In another he mocks a man who thought that his tomb would last as long as the powers of nature. In a third he describes how Virtue dwells on inaccessible rocks. But though he touches with power and charm on instructive themes, and that is no small claim, Simonides is more than a teacher. He is a poet of rare quality, who makes his effects with the utmost reticence and self-restraint. He relies for his success on the absolute rightness of his language. This gives his style a peculiar brightness, and when he uses a metaphor or simile, it comes with a sudden and dazzling brilliance, as when he compares the swift reversals of happiness to the turn of a dragon-fly's wing or speaks of a sound bursting on a great silence as " fastened to men's ears."

Behind this technique lies a great imaginative experience. Simonides has that form of sublimity which comes from concentrating on a few purified emotions. When he writes a dirge on the Greeks who fell in battle against the Persians at Thermopylæ, he uses plain words : " Of those who died at Thermopylæ glorious is the fortune and fair the doom. An altar is their tomb, for lamentation they have remembrance, and for pity praise. Such a winding-sheet decay shall not obliterate, nor all-conquering time. This sanctuary of noble men has won the glory of Hellas as its keeper." This is a severe style, but it is well suited to the moment of hushed reverence over the unconquered dead. Nor was Simonides afraid of pathos. He tells of Danaë and her child exposed in a chest at sea at night, and the mother's cry of anguish and her prayer for safety are among the masterpieces of restrained pathos in which there is no trace of the sentimental.

The defeat of the Persian invaders in 479 B.C. brought Simonides to great fame with his inscriptions for the tombs of the heroic dead. From early times metrical inscriptions had existed in Greece giving a man's name and family and perhaps some detail of his profession and achievements. They are often touching and graceful, but they are hardly poetry. The form was taken by Simonides and transformed into something that remains a marvel. The Greeks of later ages often tried to rival him, but they always failed. In two or four lines he immortalized the men of his time with the right word of praise and the just epithet. The most renowned is the epitaph on the Spartans who died at Thermopylæ. Translated, it says simply : " Stranger, tell to the Lacedæmonians that we lie here, obeying their commands." But in the original the assonances, the beat of the verses, the mixture of long and short words, make it a perfect work of art. Simonides wrote many such epitaphs, and each has its particular beauty, whether it is that of the seer who kept his place in battle though he knew it meant his death, or Archedice, the daughter, wife, and sister of princes, who never lifted up her heart to pride, or a young man who dies before marriage, or a dog whose courage is remembered in the lonely places of the mountains. He could write with a penetrating irony of a shipwrecked sailor who " came not for this but for trade " and strike with deadly aim at a slanderous poet : " After eating much and drinking much and saying much evil of men I am laid low, Timocreon of Rhodes." In this restricted and infinitely difficult medium Simonides found a perfection which demands a place among the unique successes of the Greeks. No one but he could have done it, and he did it only because he wrote in Greek.

With this particular perfection Pindar never competed, nor were his gifts of this kind. Though a Bœotian and a pupil of Corinna who wrote primitive old wives' tales in broad dialect, he saw himself as a Hellenic poet and devoted his life to expounding what he thought to be the real glories of Greece. To us he seems strangely old-fashioned and even reactionary. He cared nothing for science or democracy or for any of the high causes which Athens has bequeathed to the world. He belonged to an older order ; his life was ruled by his belief in the traditional religion and in the claims of nobility. He reverenced all that belonged to the past, and his choral odes became a magnificent survival in an age which found its characteristic art in Attic tragedy. Even in this chosen art he made few innovations. He took it as he found it and showed that its restrictions and formalities could be made to yield a peculiar beauty.

The bulk of Pindar's extant work consists of choral songs written for victors in the four great athletic festivals of Greece. These have been supplemented in recent years by fragments of Pæans, Dithyrambs, and Maiden songs, which show that whatever his subject or occasion, Pindar did not much alter his manner, and that it is no misfortune that the best preserved of his works concern boxers or chariot-drivers or runners. He exalted the occasion to his own mood, seeing athletic prowess as a god-given thing and recognizing in its possessors the blood of heroic ancestors. The games are soon forgotten in the flights of his imagination ; the transitoriness or triviality of athletic glory is transfigured by the splendid wreath he bestows. The most important men of his time attended the games, and at them Pindar met powerful patrons with whom he conversed as an equal. For their victories he wrote odes which were sung at the feasts or processions held when the victor returned home, and Pindar's poetry conveys the splendour and gaiety of these occasions.

Pindar's poetry is difficult. His abrupt transitions from one theme to another, his allusive treatment of mythology, the complicated order of his words and the difficulty of catching the exact tone of his ethical judgments, make him at first sight the most obscure of the great Greek poets. But these obstacles may be surmounted and turned into an instrument of pleasure. They take us into a special domain of fine distinctions where Greek aristocrats felt particularly at home. Pindar's work demands even a greater effort than this. He wrote for individuals, not for a standardized and anonymous posterity. The compliments he bestows or the advice he gives, the aptness of his historical allusions and his anticipations for the future, often demand an effort of the imagination to which recorded history gives little support. Some of his heroes are otherwise unknown to us, and we are left to guess the purport of the stories and lessons which Pindar gives to them.

But although at times a veil falls between us and Pindar, there remain the many intelligible beauties of his craft. Its form provides a recurring pattern into which he throws the products of his rich fancy. His adventurous collocations of words have the freshness of an art still delighting in experiment. He keeps the maxims, the myths and the personalities demanded by tradition, and impresses himself on all three. The maxims came naturally to him. He saw himself as the inspired interpreter of the Pythian Apollo, and a life devoted to the Delphic Oracle had equipped him with a store of wisdom about man's relations with the gods. He knows that man may not climb the brazen sky or go on the wonderful road to the Hyperboreans, that he must not try to be God. Herein lie the foundations of his ethics, but from this he deduces many delightful conclusions. The code he advocates for man is the temperate use of power and wealth. On this theme he speaks to his great Sicilian patrons. His code includes courtesy, forgiveness—" undying Zeus set the Titans free "—gratitude, hospitality, all the virtues possible to men who are unhampered by poverty and ready to make a generous use of their wealth.

These lessons are driven home by stories which form the central feature of nearly every ode. The virtues of kingship are illustrated by Pelops, the young prince who trusted to the gods and came to victory. Hospitality recalls the feasting in heaven when Apollo plays the lyre and the eagle nods drowsily on the sceptre of Zeus. Conversely the sin of ingratitude is illustrated by Ixion, who was tied to a wheel and thrown from heaven ; " in fetters he cannot escape he fell and proclaimed this message for all men to hear," and unfaithfulness is personified in Coronis, the girl whom Apollo loved ; she betrayed him, and he destroyed her, though he saved his unborn child from her womb. When there is no particular lesson on his mind, Pindar chooses his story for other reasons. A Rhodian boxer prompts him to tell three stories about Rhodes ; the King of Cyrene receives the Quest of the Golden Fleece ; a Corinthian runner hears of Pegasus and Bellerophon who belong to his own town. If his fancy moved him, a small hint was enough for a long story, and sometimes Pindar just put in something that charmed his fancy with no attempt at relevance, let alone at morality.

In telling his tales Pindar picks a few delightful moments and elaborates them. He assumes that all his tales are known and that what interests his hearers is his new way of telling them. He has a superb sense of details, and his narrative is a succession of separate sparkling moments. Pelops prays to Poseidon by the sea " in the darkness, alone " ; Athena springs from the head of Zeus and " Heaven shuddered at her, and mother Earth " ; Ixion lies with a cloud made in Hera's image, " fumbling a sweet lie, ignorant man " ; a Dionysian feast is held on Olympus when the cymbals of the Great Mother sound and Artemis leads in her lions from the wilderness. Pindar has, too, real powers of pathos, when he tells of the faithful brothers, Castor and Polydeuces, or of the slaughter of Cassandra by Clytæmnestra. But his greatest and most characteristic moments are of pure vision, when he passes into a paradisial radiance and writes of the child, Iamus, born among the violets, of the wedding of Cadmus and Harmonia, when the gods came as guests and the Muses sang in Thebes, of Apollo who knows how many flowers are put forth in spring, of the life of the Blessed beyond the western sea among golden flowers refreshed by gentle airs.

These glorious moments are part of Pindar's tributes of personal homage, and most of his odes close with words of praise or advice to his patrons. The praise is sometimes tedious. Lists of athletic victories can have little interest now. The advice is more interesting. Sometimes, when he speaks to the King of Syracuse about kingship or to the King of Cyrene about clemency, he finds so grand a simplicity that every word tells and the poem closes in sublime and ecstatic beauty like a symphony of Mozart. But in the end it is not the patrons who interest, but Pindar himself. His poetic personality is sustained throughout his work. He transforms all his experiences into something unique and enthralling. At times he hits out blindly at his enemies ; at times he is lost in strange apologies for his mistakes. But he has a bright vision. He knows the gods in their majesty, from Zeus, whose chariot is the lightning, to Apollo the harp-player and silver-footed Aphrodite. For him Pegasus is still stabled on Olympus, Ixion still fastened to his wheel. At times indeed he felt that all was vanity, but he soon remembered his hopes and consolations. When he was an old man, he wrote what he had always thought, and it is a fitting epitaph on his work : " Creatures of a day ! what is anyone ? what is he not ? A shadow in a dream is man. But when the god-given brightness comes, a shining light is on men, and honey-sweet days. Dear

Mother Ægina, guide this city on her voyage
of freedom, with Zeus and lord Æacus, and
Peleus, and good Telamon and Achilles."
That was the world in which he lived. All
was well when the brightness came, and at
other times man must trust to the protecting
gods. Pleasure, glory, honour, light up the
darkness in which we live, and the poet reveals their true significance to man. Though
the society which embodied his ideals decayed
and disappeared, he kept his faith to the end.

Pindar felt mainly contempt for his younger
contemporary, Bacchylides (505-450 B.C.), but
this nephew of Simonides learned his art in
a good school, and his sixteen odes show
what happened to the choral ode in other
hands. Most of the Odes are called Dithyrambs, but they have no connection with
Dionysus and hardly mention his name.
They are written for festal occasions, often,
like Pindar's, athletic. Their structure, too,
recalls Pindar's, but not their style and temper. Bacchylides' style is limpid and gay,
often beautiful with something that recalls
Simonides, an effortless clarity. He knows
how to choose his adjectives and when to loot
Homer with advantage. But he lacks Pindar's seriousness, and when he is didactic,
as he seldom is, he gives an impression of
having nothing to say. He was anxious to
please, and he succeeded ; for once at least
the King of Syracuse preferred him to Pindar
and asked him to write the ode on his victory

in the chariot-race at Olympia. His real gift is for narrative, and some of his stories have a touch of genius. He tells how Crœsus, King of Lydia, sets himself on a funeral pyre, but was rescued by Zeus and sent by Apollo to the Hyperboreans. His too is the story of the Calydonian boar-hunt and the death of Meleager. For his Athenian audience he composed two striking poems about their national hero, Theseus. In one Theseus, mocked by Minos, dives to the sea-bottom, where he sees the Nereids dancing and Amphitrite gives him a purple cloak. In the other we have something unique in Greek poetry, a dialogue between the chorus and their leader who speaks in the person of Theseus' father, Ægeus, while his son is on the way to Athens, slaying monsters and robbers. The mood is of excited expectation, and at the end comes the great peal that Athens is the hero's goal.

This poem points to a new age when the main honours fell to drama. After Bacchylides and Pindar the choral lyric ceased to count as a popular form of poetry. Its traditions were partly absorbed in the lyrical sections of the drama, partly corrupted in the new forms of the dithyramb, in which words were sacrificed more and more to music, and pretentious bombast was mistaken for the grand style. The remains of Timotheus' (c. 447-357 B.C.) *Persians* show how far the corruption went. In this welter of cheap

realism and absurd periphrasis, where the
Persians talk broken Greek and teeth are called
" marble-gleaming children of the mouth," we
can see that the fifth century had lost the
taste for the austerities and grandeurs of the
choral lyric. It belonged to an older and
more formal world.

CHAPTER III

ATTIC TRAGEDY

An ancient form of the choral dance had been that in which men disguised themselves as animals to make themselves like a god and assimilate some of his strength. The dances outlived their original purpose, and when the religion of the new wine-god, Dionysus, came to Greece in the eighth or seventh century B.C., many of them were attached to his cult, and particularly he became the master of those who, dressed as goats, had served the spirits of the woods and of the wild. He was the god of ecstatic exaltation, and he naturally became the master of all those who felt themselves in touch with nature's secrets or sought to understand the mysteries which encompass man's journey from the cradle to the grave. His rites absorbed other rites of immemorial antiquity which accompanied the great and solemn occasions in life, particularly those when man finds himself confronted by superior powers inflicting suffering and death. At Sicyon the tyrant Cleisthenes took the choruses from the local hero Adrastus and gave them to Dionysus, but before this at Corinth about 620 B.C. the poet Arion had organized the rites into a form of dramatic chorus. The dithyramb or song to Dionysus was transformed from an impromptu song into a full choric hymn with music and gesture. In time the dramatic element increased, and the chorus leader took on a character, as in Bacchylides' *Theseus*, and interchanged song with the rest of the chorus.

Such dramatic song, however, might well have remained unchanged in this form but for a peculiar combination of circumstances. In the second half of the sixth century the people of Attica began to find themselves. Under enlightened princes who patronized the arts and entertained distinguished poets from abroad, they learned to feel the need of literature as the expression of their essential character. Their taste had been trained and formed not merely by the presence of distinguished foreigners but by the annual recitation of the Homeric poems instituted by Peisistratus, and their creative energy was ready to find its own means of expression. It is characteristic that they found this not in any new form of literature but in the ancient choral dances attached to Dionysus. In the god of ecstatic excitement they saw the god of their own awakened yearnings, and in the song and dance in which he was celebrated they found the elements of an art which was to preserve and present to posterity their thoughts and feelings about the fundamental problems of humanity.

Attic tragedy began its history in the spring of 535 B.C. when at the great festival of Dionysus Thespis appeared with his chorus of *tragôdoi* or " goat-singers " and presented an elementary drama. Of his work nothing survives, but it is clear that it was not spoken but sung and was a kind of dramatic cantata. The acting was extremely simple, and only the leader had a definite part. But from these rude beginnings the Attic genius, hitherto almost inarticulate, found its characteristic poetry. Throughout the fifth century tragedy was the chief literary art at Athens, and its last triumphs coincided with the collapse of the Athenian Empire. It kept to the end the marks of its Dionysiac origin and remained both in character and structure different from the tragedy of the Renaissance and the modern world. To its association with the god it owed the preservation of the chorus, who continued to express sentiments proper to the religious consciousness. To this, too, it owed its pre-eminently serious character. Without being invariably tragic in the modern sense, it is always concerned with the great issues of life and death and especially with the relation of man to the gods. Originally a cantata which told of fearful actions but did not portray them, it avoided the representation of violent action on the stage. Death or disaster was related by a messenger, not acted before the audience's eyes. The plots were, with few and notorious exceptions, taken from saga and suited to the solemnity of the occasion at which they were performed. Tragedy remained a religious activity, even when its creators had ceased to believe in the religion to which it belonged. To it the great Athenian poets confided their deepest meditations, and in it the Athenian people found the art which touched most intimately their common consciousness and made them realize their spiritual unity.

Of early Attic tragedy nothing survives. Aristotle says that it consisted of "short myths and ridiculous language," and its products may have resembled mediæval miracle-plays. The surviving plays were written by the three tragedians whom the Greeks considered the greatest. They cover a century of development, and their variety shows of what Attic tragedy was capable. For their full appreciation they require an effort different from that given to modern tragedy. The unity of scene, the small number of actors, the stately language of set speeches, the conversations where the actors speak in alternate complete lines, the complicated choral songs, the difficult problems of religion and morality and the bland statement of homely truths, make Attic tragedy unfamiliar. But behind the austere exterior lies a world of great poetry, controlled by masterful intellects and as universal in its appeal now as it was in the great days of the fifth century.

Æschylus (525-456 B.C.) belonged to the brilliant generation which defeated the Persian invaders of 490 and 480 B.C. He fought at Marathon and had the fact recorded on his tomb to the neglect of any mention of his poetry. More than anyone he gave to Greek tragedy the form we know. He increased the number of actors from one to two ; he reduced the number of the chorus ; he made the spoken element more important than the sung. He himself was always making experiments, learning from others, improving his dramatic technique. He composed on a big scale. The unit of his art was not the single tragedy but three tragedies combined by subject into a trilogy. This was followed by another play of a half-humorous character where a heroic subject was treated with levity. But of his Satyric plays, called after their chorus dressed as satyrs, nothing survives. Æschylus worked on a plan in which the single tragedy is part of a larger scheme and must be considered in relation to the whole. The grandeur of his scale was more than matched by his poetic equipment. His vision saw a humanity transfigured by its transcendent destiny, but he pierced beyond even this heroic world to vaster and more awful shapes. He was a seer who saw into the mysteries of conflict and suffering, but he was also a poet to whom universal issues were revealed in particular symbols, formed into rhythm and design. He thought not in abstractions but in vivid images, and every word of his work shows how naturally his experiences passed into poetry. The world he created was entirely his own, as individual and as grand as that of Michelangelo. But he never lost his grip on reality or ceased to be the son of his own heroic time.

The earliest surviving play of Æschylus, the *Suppliant Women*, dates from the first decade of the fifth century. It is the first play of a trilogy, and its two sequels, the *Egyptians* and the *Daughters of Danaus*, are lost. Its archaic character may be seen in the importance of the chorus who play the chief rôle, in the simplicity of the action, in the small number of characters and in the loaded magnificence of the style. The fifty daughters of Danaus have fled with their father from Egypt to their ancestral home in Argos rather than marry their kinsmen, regarding such a union as unnatural. Such plot as there is consists of their efforts to secure protection and the arrival of a herald from Egypt announcing the presence of the rejected suitors. The action is slow and the characters not individualized. The superb and stately words do not help to differentiate one person from another, and there is a strange stiffness in the interchanges of speech. And yet the *Suppliant Women* is not merely poetry but great dramatic poetry. There is real excitement when the suppliants pray to Zeus for deliverance or shrink in horror before the

Herald's menaces. But the sustained power and appeal of the play lie in the extraordinary exaltation and excitement which pervade it and add strength to every word. If the play lacks action, it is full of passion and tenderness, and if it seems stiff or simple, it is full of inner dramatic conflict. Every line comes from a powerful vision piercing into the anxieties and torments of the characters.

The core of the *Suppliant Women* is the ethical problem which it treats. Already in it Æschylus reveals himself as finding drama and poetry in an abstract question of morality. The women who shirk all wedlock are as much to blame as the Egyptians who try to secure them by violence, and in the sequel Æschylus seems to have given his approval to the single woman, Hypermnestra, who yielded to her woman's instinct and became the ancestress of the Kings of Argos. The conflict was deep and difficult, and Æschylus treated it with great fairness and sympathy. But though this issue provides the shape of the trilogy, Æschylus did not fall into didactic or propagandist poetry. He saw the high struggle as something extremely important and exciting. Whatever the rights and wrongs might be, these were human beings concerned in it. With his prophetic insight he saw that the conflict involved human fears and desires, and with these he was properly concerned. He had perhaps his own solution, but as a dramatist and a poet he kept that till the end and made his play out of secret discords in the soul.

Between the *Suppliant Women* and the *Persians*, produced in 472 B.C., lies a great gap. The *Persians* is remarkable in many ways. It deals with an almost contemporary subject, the battle of Salamis, fought eight years before, and it has to be judged as a single play unrelated to other members of a trilogy. The scene is laid at the Persian capital of Susa, where the Elders and the Queen-Mother are full of forebodings about the fate of Xerxes and his army. A messenger brings the news of his defeat at Salamis ; the ghost of the great king Darius appears and prophesies worse to come. Then the fugitive Xerxes arrives, and the play ends with a lament between him and the chorus. The *Persians* is not tragic in the modern sense. It celebrates the heroic victory of Athens, and its core is the description of the Athenian victory. The messenger's speeches are masterpieces. Written by a man who knew what he was writing about, they lack the element of exaggeration which ruins so much martial verse. They are pæans of praise for victorious Athens. But Æschylus is fair to the enemy and gives them a grandeur in defeat. The old queen is dignified and noble, the ghost of Darius has the authority of a great king. Even Xerxes' lamentations probably seemed less unmanly to the Greeks than to us.

The success of the *Persians* lies in its style

and its temper. The majestic archaic imagery of the *Suppliant Women* has given place to something more plastic and personal. The great lines are immediately effective and convey the triumphant atmosphere of the Greeks fighting for freedom. The heroic temper is sustained through the style, and though the beauty of the closing scene is mutilated without its music, the play reaches a truly emotional climax in this collapse of a proud power. Æschylus has made poetry here out of the old theme that the gods smite the arrogant, and he leaves his verse to do its work without underlining the moral.

In the *Prometheus Bound* Æschylus leaves man for the gods. The scene is set in the deserts of Scythia, and there are no human characters. The Titan, Prometheus, has helped man by stealing fire from heaven, and the young god, Zeus, sentences him to be nailed to a mountain. The play is the first of a trilogy, and opens with Prometheus being nailed by Hephæstus and Force. When they leave him he bursts out

> " O glittering sky and breezes swift of wing,
> And river-springs, and of the ocean waves
> Innumerable laughter, mother Earth,
> And on the sun's all-seeing disk I call :
> See what, a god, I suffer from the gods."

In his solitude he is visited by the chorus of Ocean Nymphs, by Ocean himself, by the wandering Io. To these he foretells the future and explains how much he has done for man, complaining of Zeus' treatment of him. He knows that in the end Zeus will be humbled, and he has a secret which controls his doom. Hermes hears this and demands to know the secret. Prometheus refuses to tell and in a great storm and earthquake he is hurled down into Tartarus.

The *Prometheus Bound* is one of the most inspired works of man. It moves with ease in a transcendental world where issues are greater and clearer than on earth. Prometheus is the personification of the spirit ready to suffer for the good he has done, and his unyielding pride makes him more rather than less sympathetic. His character is brought out by contrast with the garrulous, time-serving Ocean and the tortured, delirious Io. His eloquent speeches are proud pieces of self-justification. He shows that his triumphant adversary Zeus is ungrateful and, like all young tyrants, abuses his power. Our sympathies and even our ethical judgments are mainly with him against Zeus, and when Shelley wrote *Prometheus Unbound* to foretell the fall of Zeus, the way was partly prepared for him by Æschylus. But it is inconceivable that in the lost *Prometheus Delivered* Æschylus provided such a conclusion. He seems to have sketched a reconciliation between Prometheus, grown humbler with suffering, and Zeus, grown less harsh with centuries of rule. The conflict he depicted was between two right causes, the betterment of humanity and the necessity of

85

order. He had seen the growth of the Athenian Empire, and he knew that every consolidation of power meant the sacrifice of some positive good. He believed that even the gods could learn and improve their ways. So he foresaw an ultimate reconciliation between the two opposed powers.

In his next surviving play Æschylus returns to the heroic age. In 467 B.C. he produced a trilogy on the sins and calamities of the House of Labdacus. The third play, the *Seven against Thebes*, survives. In this the two sons of Œdipus die in mutual combat and the accursed lineage comes to an end. But in the play the curse is kept in the background. Eteocles, the son who defends Thebes against his brother, is emphatically a soldier and a great man. He is the chief, almost the main, character. He announces the coming of war, derides the chorus of women for their cowardice, makes his dispositions to suit each arrival of news. The greater part of the play consists of scenes where he gives orders, and though they have little action, they have dramatic and descriptive beauty. Then Eteocles goes out to save the city by fighting his brother, and soon after we hear that both are dead. Here probably the play ended, and the following scene, which introduces us to the impending doom of Antigone, seems to be an addition made to bring Æschylus' conclusion into line with that of Sophocles and Euripides.

The structure of the *Seven against Thebes*

is archaic. The series of separate scenes has the stiff beauty of early sculpture or vase painting. But the play is made by the imaginative conception which pervades it. Eteocles belongs to an accursed race, and with his and his brother's death the curse ends. But Æschylus does not make him a puppet of destiny. He goes of his own accord and nobly to his doom. Heredity has not affected his character. He knows that if he does not fight his brother, his city will be captured. He has no hesitation and goes.

In 458 Æschylus produced his last work, the *Oresteia*, consisting of three plays, *Agamemnon*, *Libation Bearers*, *Eumenides*. This, the only extant trilogy, was considered by Swinburne to be " on the whole the greatest spiritual work of man." It shows us Æschylus' powers at their greatest, though he is still learning his craft, and the extra actor and the painted scenery introduced by Sophocles are both employed. At the age of sixty-seven Æschylus still absorbed new ideas and built them into his own characteristic form. In the *Oresteia* we can fully appreciate his methods and see how on the large scale of the trilogy he found full scope for his tragic effects.

The story is again of hereditary guilt. In the first play Agamemnon comes home victorious from the siege of Troy and is murdered by his wife Clytæmnestra. In the *Libation Bearers* their son, Orestes, avenges his father's death by killing his mother. In the *Eumenides* he is acquitted of guilt and purified. Each play has its own structure, but the whole has a masterly unity and deals with the single subject of blood being shed for blood. But the great problem is completely incorporated in the artistic whole. The characters illustrate the problem by their actions, but they are not symbols of this or that tendency. They are individuals responsible for their own destinies, and the appalling conflict which they sustain comes from the clash of their wills. Such lessons as may be explicitly taught come from the chorus, the mouthpiece of the inspired poet, or from the thoughts suggested and feelings stirred by the presentation of actions.

These three plays are more dramatic than the other surviving plays of Æschylus. The *Agamemnon* begins with the watchman waiting on the palace-roof for the beacon announcing the capture of Troy. He has been there for ten years, and when he sees the flare his joy lasts only a moment because he knows of the awful secret in the house—the guilty love of Clytæmnestra for Ægisthus while her husband is away. The note of suspicion and impending retribution breathes through the great choruses, and the magnificent effrontery of Clytæmnestra allays but does not dispel it. Agamemnon arrives and is forced by his wife's words to walk on a purple carpet in defiance of the moderation a conqueror should show. He goes into the palace, and his captive Cassandra foretells his death in a scene of heart-breaking pathos. Then the cries of the dying king are heard, and Clytæmnestra comes out and proclaims what she has done.

In the great scenes of the *Agamemnon* Æschylus achieves truly dramatic effects. In the *Libation Bearers* he begins with a recognition-scene between Orestes, who has been an exile since childhood, and his sister Electra. The scene is simple and lacks the sophisticated deftness of later dramas. It is followed by a long antiphonal duet where Orestes and Electra call on their father's ghost to help in the work of revenge. The scene, of tense poetical power, seems undramatic until it is clear that only with such supernatural help can Orestes kill his mother. Then the catastrophe comes quickly. Orestes meets his mother and after short and indescribably painful words kills her. The strain is too much for him, but before his reason goes he protests that he has acted rightly.

The problem implicit in the drama is whether Orestes was right to kill his mother, and if so, what end is to come to the endless cry of blood for blood. The first two plays state the problem through the characters' action and the comment of the chorus. In the *Eumenides* a solution is found. The Furies, urged on by Clytæmnestra's ghost, clamour for the death of Orestes. Trusting to

Apollo he comes to his trial and is acquitted, and the trilogy closes with a rapturous hymn declaring the transformation of the Furies into beneficent deities who protect Athens. The conclusion is perhaps more religious than ethical. The Furies belong to an old world that is passing before the new world of Apollo and Athena, the patron deities of Athens, but they are not superseded. The Furies were the old protectors of law and are as much needed as ever, though a more beneficent conception of order has come into being.

In the *Oresteia* Æschylus may fairly be judged as a dramatist. He has passed beyond the lyrical or recitative limitations of his other plays. Here he presents violent action on the stage and suits his language to it. The dying Agamemnon cries out in simple and terrible words ; the watchman uses homely figures of speech ; Orestes' sentences get tangled when he feels he is going mad. The style has lost none of its power, but it has become more flexible and follows more the needs of the dramatic situation. A similar growth may be seen in the characters. They are no longer mere types of heroic grandeur. Every word of Clytæmnestra's rings true to her character, and after death her characteristic pride and incisiveness do not leave her. Harder than Lady Macbeth and more masterful, she has her tender moments, her memory of her sacrificed daughter, her faltering in her son's presence, but the lust for revenge has frozen her into a murderess. The humbler characters, such as the Watchman or Orestes' nurse, garrulous and pathetic, or Electra, the lonely brooding daughter of a dishonoured home, are perfectly conceived and real. Æschylus also extracts a peculiar beauty from the situation in which he places a character. We know nothing of the Herald who brings the news of Agamemnon's arrival, but his words are the right expression of a mood which follows the conclusion of a great effort when memory becomes sweet and a man is ready to die. When Cassandra stands before Agamemnon's door and foretells his and her own death, there is no need to delineate her personality. Her tragic situation is entirely sufficient, and her last words the right comment on it.

" Ah, for the life of man ! In happiness
    It may be like a shadow—in unhappiness
    A wet sponge drips and blots the picture out."

Æschylus took cantata and turned it into tragedy, making it the vehicle of his imaginative experience. He thought profoundly and originally about human destiny, and his dramas were the mirror of his thoughts, but his thoughts concerned man, and he saw man in the light of a great vision. So sharp was his sight and so human his judgment that his creatures are never puppets. Caught in a cosmic plan they remain living and individual, abating none of their eloquence and none of their vitality. They even make their own destinies. They are free to choose, and their choice decides their end. Æschylus is a liberator, who resolved the discords of religion without undermining religion itself. His religion made him a poet, and his unreckonable gifts of speech, his surprising and potent metaphors, his sudden stark outbursts, his moments of grace and tenderness, his control of the supernatural and the terrifying, were the gifts of the god who spoke through him to the people and made him the instrument of his revelation.

Sophocles (495–406 B.C.) sang as a boy in the choir of thanksgiving for Salamis. His life coincided with the greatest days of Athens, and he died before its capture. In his life and his work he has come to stand as a symbol for the Periclean age, and in many senses he is its true representative. A man of moderate opinions, attached to religion and morality, he lived in sympathy with his time, consorting easily with the greatest and respected by all. But he was also a poet, who continued the work of Æschylus by portraying on the stage problems suggested by the relation of man with the gods. He found the traditional form congenial, and though he made many technical improvements, he kept within the proper limits of his art and observed the accepted tone of tragedy. He found the trilogy not to his taste and composed on the smaller scale of the single play. He increased the number

struggle in her between tenderness and jealousy, her anxiety to win back her husband's love, though she hardly knows him, show new triumphs of Sophoclean art. From Heracles she has got nothing, and even when he hears of her death, he has no words of pity. So far the play is entirely human and natural, written with great care and knowledge. Then, when the horror is greatest, when Deianira is dead and Heracles is wasting away in torture from the fatal shirt of Nessus, the tone changes. Heracles realizes that his death is near, that all his labours are ended. In words of growing confidence and command he tells his son to prepare his funeral pyre on Mount Œta. He must fulfil an oracle foretelling his death, and nothing must stand in his way.

This conclusion is strange, and there is some awkwardness in the shifting of interest from Deianira to Heracles. But the plan is there. Heracles is the embodiment of heroic manhood, on whom the gods have laid burdens all his life. Therefore he stands outside ordinary human claims, even outside his poor wife's tragedy. But the Greeks knew that in the end he was received among the gods, and so, when Sophocles prepares us for his death, it is for an apotheosis, a reward for all that he has suffered. And this reward atones even for Deianira's death. Her appalling mistake was not a mistake after all but part of the divine plan to release Heracles from his labours.

Sophocles finds his solution in this passing of the hero into godhead, and when such events happen, it is not for man to criticize the means.

And yet this conclusion is not entirely satisfactory. The man in Sophocles was stronger than the moralist, and the *Women of Trachis* ends on a note of questioning, almost of complaint. The young son of Heracles and Deianira speaks of the deaths and sufferings which have come to pass and says " there is not one of them which is not Zeus." It looks as if Sophocles' acceptance of the divine will was not so contented as when he wrote the *Ajax*, as if he saw that an appeal to faith was not enough. There still remained unresolved discords and a sense of the injustice of the gods. He had presented the conflict between them and man, and he was unable to justify its conclusion. Though he remained religious to the end and deeply attached to the ceremonies and cults of Athens, he came more and more to realize that the orthodox explanation of suffering was narrow and hard-hearted, that it left out of account our sympathy for humanity. In each play after the *Women of Trachis* he probes the dark places of tragedy, and in each he finds some ultimate clash between man and circumstance. He gave no overt explanation and left the ways of God unjustified, but as a poet he found his solution. He saw that in the grip of inevitable disaster man becomes his noblest self, and that was enough for him.

The result of these inner changes was revealed in *King Œdipus*. Written in the first years of the war between Athens and Sparta, the play bears the mark of the dark days when plague devastated Athens. It is entirely and essentially tragic, the story of a great man hunted and trapped by fate. Admired by Aristotle as the perfect tragedy, it keeps all its original power, and whether we consider its plot or its style or its characterization or its poetry, it remains unchallenged. Œdipus has heard an oracle that he will marry his mother and kill his father. He takes every step to avoid his fate, only to find years later that he has done what the oracle foretold. The play is concerned with his discovery of the truth and with his blinding of himself because of it. Sophocles spares nothing in the relentless sweep of events and the appalling catastrophe to which they lead. Every scene is a stage which brings Œdipus nearer to the truth, and even apparent moments of hope are pregnant with more deadly disaster. The great man, resourceful, courageous, singularly honest, is driven by his own character into making further and further inquiries, and when he finds the truth, he breaks down and blinds himself.

In *King Œdipus* Sophocles writes tragedy in the modern sense. His Œdipus has his faults or at least the defects of his great qualities. His hasty temper and masterful rapidity of action have perhaps marked him out for trouble, but the actual disaster which befalls him is undeserved and outside his control. Even his blinding of himself, shocking as it was to Greek ideas, was dictated by a desire to escape from the intolerable burden of almost physical guilt. He is essentially tragic because in his fight against insuperable odds he shows all his nobility of character and is none the less defeated. The other characters are fit companions for him—the old seer Teiresias, anxious to hide the truth but forced into telling it; Creon, mechanical and honourable; Jocasta, entirely a woman, whose chief aim is to keep Œdipus happy, no matter what the truth may be. All are caught in the tense excitement and deadly horror. The play opens with a plague-stricken people calling to Œdipus for help, and ends with him, blind, deprived of his daughters and faced with exile. But perhaps the greatest moment in the play, indeed in all Greek tragedy, is that when Jocasta realizes that she is married to her own son and goes into the palace to kill herself, saying

" Alas, accursèd one ! That name alone
    I give to you, and nothing ever more."

The dark years of the war left their mark in a different way on the *Electra*. The subject is that of Æschylus' *Libation Bearers,* but Sophocles treats it entirely in his own way.

His concern is less with Orestes than with his sister, Electra. In her sorrow and loneliness, her brooding over past injuries and her hopes for her brother's return, Sophocles found the core of his drama. The action consists of the news of Orestes' death, his arrival, and the exacting of vengeance on Clytæmnestra and her lover. The play is written with great brilliance, and in the scene where Electra weeps over the supposed ashes of her brother it reaches a strange and unexpected pathos. Sophocles makes no attempt to grapple with the great issues raised by Æschylus. He takes the story as the saga knew it. What interests him is not its ethical significance but what the characters felt and thought. In a story like this such treatment might seem at first a little hard-hearted. Neither Clytæmnestra nor her lover seems to receive fair play. The truth is that with the growing barbarism of the war Sophocles had come to understand revenge and the hardness of heart which comes from long brooding over injuries. In Electra all love for her mother has died, and in Orestes desire for revenge has been fanned to an all-consuming passion by the old servant who has brought him up to this single end. The play is a study in these dark passions. It is almost objective drama, free of religious or ethical intention. Sophocles seems to have asked himself what happened and to have written his play as the answer.

Sophocles continued writing in extreme old

age, and two plays survive to show that when he was over eighty his powers had not flagged. The *Philoctetes*, produced in 409 B.C., has not a tragic conclusion but is concerned with essentially tragic issues. It is an acute, exciting, and painful study of three characters in conflict with each other and with themselves. The story turns on the attempt to bring to Troy the hero, Philoctetes, who has been abandoned for ten years on a desolate island. In the character of Philoctetes Sophocles reveals a new phase of his art. The solitary castaway, whose life has been broken by sickness and continual hardship, is still a great man, noble, generous, honourable. But he has brooded for years over his injuries, and he cannot forget or forgive the wrongs done to him by Odysseus. The plot consists of the attempt made by Odysseus through Neoptolemus, the young son of Achilles, to trick Philoctetes by lies into coming to Troy. Odysseus himself is a type which war brings to power. He understands reasons of state and little else, but for these he will make any sacrifice of honour and charity. He appeals to Neoptolemus' ambition and sense of duty, and for a time all goes well. Neoptolemus shows himself a capable liar and is on the point of bringing Philoctetes with him to Troy when all breaks down. The open-hearted friendship of Philoctetes touches the young soldier's heart and he tells the truth. His natural nobility triumphs over his ambition and sense of discipline. Then the three characters are confronted in an insoluble conflict. Philoctetes knows that Odysseus wants him, and nothing will make him yield a jot of his hostility. Odysseus can thunder and bluster, but he remains impotent, and nothing can deaden the revived humanity of Neoptolemus, who has promised his friendship to Philoctetes and keeps his word. The problem is only solved by divine intervention.

The *Philoctetes* is perhaps not a completely successful play. The conclusion is almost a confession that the plot has become too complicated to be solved by ordinary means. But of all Sophocles' plays it shows perhaps the finest psychological insight and the strongest grasp of the conflicts which rage in great men. To these dramatic elements almost everything is sacrificed. There are no messenger's speeches; the choric songs are unimportant. Almost every line goes to delineate the drama that is taking place in the characters, and every line tells. In this world of angry passions and conflicting motives Sophocles reveals something truly tragic and touching. Honour is menaced by utility or corrupted by long injuries. The degradation and misery of war form the background against which these tortured figures move, and though the end is in a sense happy, and angry words are lost in a divine calm, the main impression left is that Sophocles has once again been carried beyond his theme and found in the old story dark and dangerous elements for which there was no orthodox apology. His main interest lay in the characters and what they felt, and to these he brought an unflinching analysis and a sense of tragic values, which overrode the traditional moral of the tale.

In his last play, *Œdipus at Colonus*, Sophocles was partly concerned with the same angry passions as in the *Philoctetes*, but his treatment of them is entirely different. The old blind Œdipus comes to Attica, knowing that it is his last resting-place and that the protecting presence of his body will help Athens for ever. Despite the loyal companionship of his daughters and the chivalrous welcome given to him by the Athenian king, Theseus, even this last act is made difficult for Œdipus, and the first part of the play is concerned with the obstacles he finds in the countrymen who are horrified at him and in Creon who tries to secure by fraud or violence his protection for Thebes instead of Athens. But these fierce scenes are transcended in the miraculous close where Œdipus, led by no helping hand, hears a voice calling from heaven and passes into the earth, confident and unseen. In Colonus his body was said to rest, and with such comfort did Sophocles tend Athens in the last days of the Peloponnesian War, turning attention away from the appalling present to the country-side and its immemorial sanctities.

In this play Sophocles makes it abundantly clear that Œdipus is in no sense to blame for what he has done and that his expulsion from Thebes was an act of callous cruelty. His end is the atonement for his sufferings, and perhaps in it Sophocles saw the solution of the question which had troubled him all his life; through suffering, even through the injustice done to him, the great man becomes a god. But the play treats of deeper questions even than this. The angry scenes where Œdipus upbraids Creon or curses his own son, Polynices, rise from the very loyalty and feeling of comradeship which Sophocles valued so highly and which seemed to be disappearing under the strain of the war. Œdipus rewards those who help him, but for those who have treated him wrongly, he has not forgiveness but righteous anger. Sophocles had seen enough of civil strife to know that it struck at the roots of society and that for certain forms of disloyalty forgiveness is useless and undeserved. In a world where life is of little worth, what counts most is constancy and friendship. Œdipus, buried in the soil of Attica, remains loyal to those who helped him at the last, and it was not for the others who insulted and expelled him to expect his supernatural protection.

There is much that is strange in *Œdipus at Colonus*, much too that is painful. When the Chorus sings in words of unsurpassable eloquence of the misery of old age and the uselessness of life, or when Œdipus tells Theseus that

"Faith dies and unfaith blossoms like a flower," [1]

Sophocles, the renowned embodiment of Attic calm, throws aside all reserve and shows that he understood the vanity of things as well as Shakespeare. But for this half-hidden despair he has his own consolations, which he embodies in the devoted loyalty of Antigone, the quick understanding of Theseus, and above all in the beauties of the country-side where he was born, in that Colonus where the nightingale sings and narcissus and crocus bloom, where Dionysus walks with the Nymphs and the Muses accompany Aphrodite. The ties which bound Sophocles to his own land were in the end the strongest, and he saw in the last hours of Œdipus a parable of those loyalties which hold men together in their darkest hours and are a priceless gift from the gods.

To his contemporaries Sophocles was the perfect Athenian, contented with his age and with his art. So perhaps he was in his ordinary life, but this marmoreal conception of him can only distort our judgment of his work. He was primarily a poet, who found his material in the sufferings and conflicts of men and used every resource of a matchless style and a great dramatic sense to turn these discords into poetry. His first concern was with man; he saw his characters from inside and

[1] Trs. G. Murray.

transfused them with real life, exalting them to that special state of vividness which only poetry can give. If he did not propound great solutions of cosmic difficulties, it was not because he was uninterested or incapable. Over these problems he thought hard and long, but the record of his thought is to be found not in explicit statement but in the way he created his characters. His appeal was not through demonstration to the intellect but through poetry to the emotions. With great power and resource he showed where exactly the conflict lay, but he left all answers and all ethical or religious judgments to his hearers. He was before everything an artist, but an artist who knew that no issue was too difficult or too great for his art, who saw that discords beyond the reach of the intellect may be solved through the heart.

Euripides (480–406 B.C.) was only fifteen years younger than Sophocles, but he belonged to a different generation. Between them lies the chasm of the Sophistic Movement. The Sophists were professional teachers who applied new methods of criticism to all aspects of life. Among them were men of the highest intellectual powers and originality. There were also men of lesser gifts and even of suspected sincerity. But the effects of the movement were incalculable. The traditional and ordered life of Athens was subjected to acute analysis, and inevitably many accepted notions were discredited. Scientific in its origins, the movement invaded many sides of life. It concerned itself with physics and art, with religion and morality. It created a taste for new ideas ; it completely altered the intellectual life of Athens and deeply affected the drama.

Of this movement Euripides was the child. It made him a sceptic and a critic. It affected his whole attitude towards life and made it impossible for him to accept the presuppositions of tragic art as his great predecessors had accepted them. He was driven to write tragedy because he had something to say, because he was a poet, because only through tragedy could he reach a large audience. But he was largely out of sympathy with its religious setting, and his agnosticism saw the Olympian gods more as devils than as mythological fantasy. He seems even to have lacked a consistent philosophy of his own, to have been always accepting and then abandoning new ideas. To some extent his plays are the record of his spiritual wanderings, revealing him as testing the effectiveness of every theory and finding a home in none. His changes of standpoint and his temporary acceptance of ideas which now seem curiously unsubstantiated deprive his work of the timeless claims of Æschylus and Sophocles. He lacks a background and a stable personality. And yet he is not only a man of the greatest interest. He is also a poet who gave to tragedy something which hitherto it had only possessed in a small measure.

Euripides approached tragedy entirely from the point of view of man. In so far as he was concerned with the gods, he saw them as blind and unreasonable powers of nature, often destructive and deadly. His interest was in human beings, and his contribution to his art lay in the wide vision and acute understanding which he possessed of men and women. He was a psychologist who allowed himself no limits and therefore saw further and perhaps deeper than Sophocles. Undeterred by the traditional nobility of tragedy he did not confine himself to the sufferings of the great. He tried to make all humanity his field and to find his subjects in characters hitherto neglected or scorned. For this he was well qualified not merely by his natural curiosity and intelligence but also by a remarkably sensitive and sympathetic heart. His pity was deeply stirred by much that would have left others cold or escaped ordinary notice. The informing spirit of this art lies in this pity and insight. Moved by them he approached the problems of tragedy and gave them a new treatment and perhaps a new solution.

His first two plays, *Cyclops* and *Alcestis* (438 B.C.), show a poet who has found himself and his style. *Cyclops* is a Satyr play and retells a famous episode from the *Odyssey*. It has not merely a wistful beauty when it tells of the Cyclops' pastoral life. It has also a new sense of personality. The Cyclops is certainly like Homer's Polyphemus, but Euripides has developed his character and filled in the details of Homer's sketch. He is of course drunken, lecherous and bestial, but he is more than that. He has a certain gaiety and even poetry in him. He is a child of nature, and Euripides somehow manages to understand him. *Alcestis* was acted instead of a Satyr play and is in no sense a tragedy, but it indicates in what direction Euripides' mind had begun to move. A king is saved from death because his wife consents to die for him, and the wife is brought back from the grave by Heracles. To the old story, half-sentimental and half-humorous, Euripides brings a variety of gifts. The pathos of the dying queen and the interposition of the drunken Heracles reveal a dramatist who knew how to make the most of his situations. But to its audience, who expected a lesson on the heroism of a wife who dies for her husband, *Alcestis* must have given a slight shock. Euripides keeps strictly to the story, but his understanding of the characters upsets the traditional balance. The king, Admetus, who should be noble and heroic, is made inferior and ridiculous by his selfish insistence on his wife dying for him and his self-pity after her death. He is only saved from complete discredit by Heracles. The pleasant old tale had been given a new turn, and it was clear

that Euripides approached tradition with a
fresh mind.

The subjects of Greek tragedy had to
be drawn from the heroic age, and such a
limitation might well have inhibited Euripides' modern and progressive mind. But he
accepted the limitation and treated the old
stories afresh, asking himself what permanent
truth lay in them. The result was a series of
plays dealing with notorious women of antiquity. In *Medea* (431 B.C.), *Hippolytus* (428
B.C.), *Hecuba* (c. 424 B.C.), and *Andromache*
(c. 422 B.C.) Euripides produced a series of
tragic studies in womanhood which appalled
and delighted his audiences. By disregarding
the proprieties and overriding the conventional view of women, he created something
entirely new in these intimate, accurate, merciless and yet completely sympathetic studies of
violent lost souls. His heroines are far from
Antigone or Deianira, and yet in spite of their
all too human weaknesses and their outbursts
of sheer savagery, they are essentially tragic.
For Euripides part of their interest lay in the
conflict he found in them. In Medea he depicted the struggle between a mother's love
for her children and a flouted wife's desire for
revenge on her husband, in Phædra unlawful
love struggling for expression against ingrained
habit, in Hecuba tenderness being turned to
savagery by suffering, and in Andromache a
princess broken by captivity to accept what
the gods send. In each case the conflict in

the chief character is mirrored in the external conflict round them, and each plot is concerned with the clash of competing wills and even of irreconcilable characters. The object of Phædra's passion is the pure Hippolytus who abhors all love, and Hecuba is confronted with Odysseus whose hard heart is unmoved by her tragic pathos. In each case the issue is painful, and unless the gods intervene, there is no solution but disaster and death.

In these plays Euripides created something entirely new. Their power is past question. In them there was much beside psychology to ravish his audiences—the deft, silken style, the flights of song moving with airy grace, the painter's eye which adds such colour to the descriptive speeches, the great and genuine power of the high dramatic moments when Medea talks to her children before killing them or Phædra declares the love she wishes to conceal. There were indeed other characteristics more suited to ancient than to modern taste. When Jason explains to Medea the advantages she has gained from living in Greece or Hippolytus suggests that the gods should never have created women or Hecuba wrangles with her conquerors, they seem to fall below tragic dignity, but to the supporters of Euripides this was a delightful realism which brought home the real meaning of the old stories. But there were still other characteristics which made even his supporters uneasy. Euripides paid lip-service to religion.

The gods are invoked in choruses, and the source of each legend is appropriately acknowledged in local custom or tradition. But the religious tone rings false. In *Hippolytus* Aphrodite strikes down Hippolytus because he neglects her, and Artemis, to whom his life is dedicated, can do nothing for him when he is dying. These may be great powers of nature, beyond good and evil, but they are not the acknowledged objects of worship. In *Andromache* Apollo, for whom Euripides felt a particular aversion, betrays Neoptolemus to his death at Delphi. There is no overt criticism, still less anything resembling blasphemy, but the orthodox Athenian must have felt uneasy at the unfamiliar light thrown on the actions of the gods.

The truth is that Euripides was primarily concerned with man and regarded the gods as fictions or powers of nature or destructive illusions. His moral nature was revolted by some of the legends about them, and he preferred to find his solutions elsewhere than in an acceptance of the divine will. In *Heracles* (*c*. 422 B.C.) and *Electra* (*c*. 413 B.C.) he took two stories deeply tinged with traditional religion and re-stated them in his own way. His *Heracles* is a study of the hero who kills his children in a fit of madness, but instead of treating it as a punishment for pride Euripides makes the madness undeserved and unexplained, a rift in the universe, and closes the play with a scene of great moral beauty where Theseus purifies the recovered Heracles and acquits him of his guilt. In *Electra* he takes up the familiar story and makes the desire for revenge a form of morbid aberration. Where Æschylus explains and Sophocles accepts, Euripides understands and condemns. He shows how Orestes and Electra are driven into murdering their mother, but he shows too that their action and the principles it invokes are horrible. By making the murdered mother an ordinary human being he brings home the ghastly depravity of matricide. When the murder is done, there is no satisfaction for the murderers.

The great power of these two plays, genuinely tragic and powerful, shows one side of Euripides' personality. Concurrently with them he wrote other plays in which the main interest is political. In the first years of the Peloponnesian War he was an ardent supporter of the Athenian cause and shared the belief of Pericles that Athens was the school of Hellas and a city for whom it was an honour to die. In his *Sons of Heracles* he dealt with the hospitality once offered by Athens to the founders of Sparta and recalled bygone kindnesses shown to the present enemy. The *Suppliant Women* is a study in his ideal city. In Theseus he presents the perfect leader, the man who gives full rights and liberty to all. The play concerns the rights of burial and has hardly plot or characters, only a beautiful and poetical presentation of a great city under a

great king. Its exalted nobility of tone keeps
the action in a heroic age, but its sentiments
must have stirred many of his contemporaries
to think that this was true of Athens in their
own day.

Like that of Thucydides and Sophocles, Euripides' patriotism was less ardent and confident when the war began again. His *Trojan
Women* (415 B.C.) is a terrible study of the
great women of Troy after its capture, waiting
for death or enslavement. Here too there is
little plot, and the main character is the
chorus who tell in wonderful words of the
woes of war and slavery. Even Hecuba and
the pathetic prophetess, Cassandra, seem members of the chorus made more personal and
articulate. In this truly tragic play Euripides
reveals the bitter experiences of war, and it
is notable that he had few illusions about the
value of victory. For him war has become
senseless and useless cruelty, as demoralizing
for the conquerors as it is deadly for the con-
quered. It is significant of his courage and
insight that he produced the *Trojan Women* in
415 B.C. the year of the fatal Athenian expedition to Sicily. The dark shadow of the
war lies also over the *Phœnician Women* (*c.*
410 B.C.), in which Euripides took the theme
of Æschylus' *Seven against Thebes* and trans-
posed to the remote past a burning problem
of contemporary history, the fierce intestine
strife which raged in every Greek city and
broke old loyalties and domestic ties. The

picture he presents of might in conflict with right, of unchecked and ruthless ambition, of general demoralization, is drawn from the life he saw and fits awkwardly into the heroic setting. The limits of tragic art had become too narrow for the poet's feelings.

The active, analytical mind which so probed the weaknesses of politics was also busy on religion. In *Ion* (*c.* 420 B.C.) Euripides continued his studies of the gods. His heroine is a woman who has been raped by Apollo and then abandoned, and the plot turns on her discovery of her child by him whom she abandoned years before. The play is painful, even savage. The heroine, Creusa, denounces Apollo in words of hate and vengeance, and though our sympathies are with her, Euripides is careful to let us see how suffering has demoralized and embittered her character. If his purpose was merely to discredit Apollo, his art carried him far beyond it, and his *Ion* is built out of perfectly real, if ugly, passions. In *Orestes* (408 B.C.) he combined an ethical and psychological question with pure melodrama. The story is that of Orestes pursued by Furies, and Euripides characteristically makes the Furies mere creatures of Orestes' guilty and disordered fancy. The first scenes probe this dark problem, but then the tone changes ; the play turns to conspiracy and violence and ends with a dramatic curtain, as if Euripides felt that he had gone too far and must get back to mere drama.

There was however in Euripides another strain, curiously consorted with his realism, a strain of romantic and lyrical joy, which found an outlet in his choric songs and in *Hippolytus*, but reached a second flowering in the later years of the war when ugly realities turned him back to worlds of fancy. In *Iphigeneia in Tauris* (c. 413 B.C.) it is true that Orestes is still pursued by phantoms and that Apollo is still a villain, but the action takes place at the end of the world among barbarians who sacrifice strangers, and the grimness is lost in songs full of the sea and in the delicious and exciting scenes where the Greeks escape from their captors. In *Helen* (412 B.C.), written perhaps to console Athens after the disaster at Syracuse, Euripides has passed beyond problems. It is a fairy-tale built on the story of Stesichorus that Helen never went to Troy but stayed in Egypt. Full of delightful songs and of a gracious element of comedy, it touches no tragic emotion, and seems to be mainly concerned with the power of a beautiful and clever woman to extricate men from the troubles in which they find themselves. Helen triumphs over the blustering Egyptian king and over her own conceited and stupid husband. In her Euripides has created a character wonderfully fresh and charming, a symbol of what sense and sweetness can do when power has failed.

Before the end of the war Euripides left

Athens and found a last home in Macedon. There he wrote a play, *The Bacchants*, in which all his powers were combined at their best. In it he is concerned with Dionysus, the power of wine and ecstatic religion, a real power of nature, indifferent to good or evil and destructive of all who oppose him. In the story of the King of Thebes who defies Dionysus and because of it is hypnotized by him and torn to pieces by his own mother, Euripides has written something infinitely tragic and even horrible but full too of a grim humour and of a deep feeling for the magic and mystery of nature. As a poet he understands the inhuman excitement which fills the Bacchants and as a thinker he sees how destructive this ecstatic fervour is. But he welds the different elements into a perfect whole, where every scene is intensely exciting and every song beautiful. He was no longer tilting against phantoms. He was concerned with something real and terrible, and from the fatal conflict of a man with this superhuman and amoral power he made a tragedy that suited all his gifts. With this and *Iphigeneia in Aulis*, an unfinished play full of grace and tenderness, Euripides ended his life.

Unlike Sophocles, Euripides followed no single line of development, and his art is the record of his many interests. Controversial in his own life, he has remained controversial for posterity, and the value of his work still provokes dispute. He brought to poetry some unexampled gifts, a glittering style, a natural sense of melody, a great sense of the dramatic, an insight into character, especially into the unusual and the misunderstood. But his nature made it almost impossible for him to be at ease with tragedy. He tried to vary its character with new expedients, and not all were successful. His exhibitions of sophistical rhetoric, his slick apophthegms, his delight in archaic forms like an explanatory prologue or the solution of a plot by a god's intervention, his desire to insert allusions to contemporary events, all these delighted his friends, but to us they are mainly of historical interest. There was too a discord in him which made it difficult for him to create a harmonious whole. One part of him was romantic and lyrical, enchanted by old stories and accepting even the gods as a pretty fancy, content with an almost visible beauty found in the past and capable of a rare and exquisite longing. The other part was critical and realistic, demanding that solid reality should be presented in the drama and that serious problems should be discussed. Sometimes, as in *Hippolytus* and *The Bacchants*, the two sides were harmoniously united, and the realism gave weight and strength to a great imaginative conception. At other times the discord is visible, and plays possessing great beauties are marred by sudden harsh notes. But in spite of everything Euripides remains " the most tragic of the poets " because he saw tragedy as an entirely human thing, and with great insight and power he depicted men and women suffering, but attempted no lesson or consolation. The writing of tragedy was his concern, and though he undermined its traditional character and made many experiments with it, he succeeded not once but often in presenting situations so pathetic and terrible that he was rightly classed with Æschylus and Sophocles, a fit companion for the immortals.

CHAPTER IV

THE DEVELOPMENT OF HISTORY

THE use of prose for literature is usually later than that of verse, and, if we except the early codes of law, the first appearances of Greek prose are scientific, and none are earlier than the sixth century. Even of this prose only scattered sentences remain, and few have any literary interest. Heraclitus of Ephesus (fl. 500 B.C.) indeed combined a relentlessly critical mind with a philosophy of universal flux, presenting his thoughts in apophthegms of oracular magnificence. In his concentrated maxims a powerful, ironical intellect is at work; when he says tersely that " war is the father of all things " or " the learning of many things does not teach understanding," it is plain that his words have been wrung out of him by bitter experience, and that he is turning prose to other objects than mere instruction. He can claim to be judged as an artist, but most of the early prose-writers were concerned only to make themselves clear, and their style was eminently serviceable. Their work paved the way for others who should combine clarity with a sense of those other appeals which well-written prose makes to its readers.

121

The growth of science in Ionia, though primarily directed towards physics, meant that sooner or later men must look at man and ask questions about him. For centuries natural interest and curiosity in the past had been satisfied by the epic, which claimed to tell the truth and to be concerned with great doings. But the appearance of a scientific spirit meant that neither could all that the epic said be accepted as gospel nor could the scientist well record his own discoveries in heroic verse. Elements of prose history existed in the collections of myths and genealogies made for patrons interested in their family-trees, but there was no history in the modern sense until the conflict with Persia stirred Greek curiosity to ask what manner of men were these who had threatened civilization and Greek pride, to record the victory over an apparently vast power. The first real history was written by Hecatæus of Miletus (fl. 500 B.C.) who announced : " What I write here is the account which I considered to be true. For the stories of the Greeks are numerous and in my opinion ridiculous." His work seems primarily to have been a geography, but he included much that belongs to history. His approach to his subject was critical and rationalist. He criticized the myths of the past and he tried to tell the truth about his own age. He established truth instead of amusement as the object of history.

His work however was completely eclipsed

by Herodotus (c. 484–425 B.C.). The "father of history" is the true child of this scientific tradition. His work is *historiê*, "inquiry," and his opening words declare his aim: "This is the publication of the inquiry of Herodotus of Halicarnassus, that neither may the achievements of men be blotted out by time nor may great and marvellous doings, some done by Greeks, some by foreigners, lose their fame, both other things and why they fought with each other." This declaration is in the spirit of the Ionian scientists. It lacks any mention of ethical instruction or of literary ambition. It is studiously impartial —the foreigner is to be considered equally with the Greek. The limpid style proclaims its affinities with scientific writing. The subject of the Persian Wars is treated as a natural phenomenon and approached in appropriate terminology.

The claim of Herodotus is that he formulated the nature of history and that his work shows how well he conceived its character. To the scientists he owed his style and his conception of history as a series of events. But he was dealing with men, and for them science gave him little help. He turned instead to the epic, his forerunner in historical narrative. His subject had been raised to poetic dignity by Simonides and Æschylus, and his unquestioning sense of its greatness prompted him to conceive it as an epic theme. To the epic he owes his wide canvas and free method of narrative, his portraiture of great men, his use of speeches and debates, the spirit of his battle-scenes, his sense of divine supervision and even of divine interposition. The " great and marvellous doings " would in an earlier age have been celebrated in poetry, and Herodotus saw himself as continuing the tradition under new conditions of prose and science.

At intervals he shows other influences. Some of his stories smack of the professional story-teller and have the spice and sting of the market-place. Once at least, in his account of the death of Crœsus' son, his manner is modelled closely on tragedy and secures its effect through an unexpected reversal of fortune. But these are small variations in the general scheme. Herodotus had not the later notion of history as a unity where event follows event in logical and chronological order. His aim is nothing less than to depict the rival worlds of Greek and Persia which eventually met in conflict. Therefore he constructs his book on loose lines, giving full play to the many influences and personalities which seem relevant. Seeing the Persian Wars as the culmination of an age-old rivalry between East and West, he naturally went far afield in his studies, and his history covers all that he thought pertinent to his scheme. He was moreover a pioneer, and his natural delight in discovery made him put down much that a relentless self-criticism might have omitted. But though in its beginnings his work seems diffuse, its plan is gradually unfolded. Herodotus depicts on a liberal scale the world before the Persian Wars. There is a great variety in this and an apparent lack of cohesion, because the conditions of his work forced Herodotus to put into his text what might better have gone into footnotes, appendices, and even maps. But all is pulled together by the conflict in which the opposed worlds meet. Once the war begins there is a great sweep of narrative which carries us on to the end.

Herodotus had an omnivorous curiosity. He was an incomparable " picker-up of unconsidered trifles," and the range of his information is enormous both in time and place. His stories go back to Minos, even to the Fourth Dynasty of Egypt. He preserves echoes of the Hittite and Assyrian Empires. He travelled far for his time, visiting the Black Sea, Egypt and Babylon, and collected stories of the caravan route to the Niger, of Phœnicians sailing round Africa, of burial customs in Central Asia, of Indians who ate their parents. From the Black Sea he gathered a full account of the peoples of South Russia from the Scythians of the Crimea to the Mongols of the Urals. In Greece itself he tapped many sources of information from the instructive stories of the Delphic Oracle to the propaganda of the Athenian democracy and the official versions of Spartan history.

He absorbed the folk-memory of centuries with its vivid personalities and apt lessons, and built all the different materials into the homogeneous structure of his history.

Herodotus was not a critical historian in the modern sense. He neither researched into original documents—though if they came his way, he made use of them—nor had he mature, scientific methods of finding the truth. He was an honest man, who put down what he believed to be true and recorded doubt when he felt it. But he was also a man of his age who accepted some current ideas which posterity has discarded. He knew that the world was full of wonders, and he did not rule the miraculous out of existence. He was impressed by the tittle-tattle of Egyptian priests and by the moralizing stories which emanated from Delphi. He records portents for what they are worth, and his faith is liable to see a lesson in the fall of the great. He was deeply attached to the traditional view that the gods are jealous of human prosperity, and he enforces the doctrine with many examples. Indeed, it runs through his whole conception of the Persian Empire and is the main moral of his history. The theme, familiar in Pindar and Simonides, is exalted into a law of life.

His graver successors make some of Herodotus' effects look a little childish. His interpretation of oracles, his attribution of mundane motives, his eye for a picturesque touch, like the Spartan king who took his drink neat or the king of Lydia who thought his wife "far the most beautiful of all women," his light-hearted treatment of fierce issues, like tyranny in Athens or the causes of the Ionian Revolt, have brought down on him the thunderbolts of the graver and higher criticism. But if we consider his circumstances, this apparent childishness falls into its place. Herodotus composed not for private study but for public recitation. By reading sections of his work he made his living, and he had always to keep his audience in mind. Therefore what he tells and his manner of telling it are accommodated to the taste of people who might easily get bored or frightened by something too unfamiliar. The stories suited to such a taste were not necessarily any more untrue than if they were couched in graver tones. The motives which Herodotus sometimes imputes to the great, vanity, jealousy, fear, pride, are not less likely to be right than the strictest interpretations based on economics or world politics. They belong to the subjective side of history, and the historian is free to do what he thinks fit with them.

On the other hand, his doubts and hesitations are as instructive as his faith. He did not believe that either Heracles or Helen was the child of divine parentage. He was certainly sceptical of stories which attributed natural phenomena to the immediate action of the gods. He allows that a ravine in Thessaly may have been made by Poseidon, because Poseidon is said to produce earth-quakes, and the ravine looks like the result of an earthquake. He allows that the Athenians believe a great snake to live on the Acropolis, but he himself neither accepts nor denies the belief. He says plainly : " They present a honey-cake every month as to a creature existing." That left the question open and avoided all imputation of impiety. He had absorbed some, but by no means all, of the Ionian enlightenment. He drew no exact line between human and divine action but decided each case on its merits.

In physical matters he felt more confident and incorporated much of the science of his day. Like all science past its prime, this equipment looks a little odd now, and Hero-dotus is easily shown to be wrong when he postulates a law of geographical symmetry which makes the Nile flow parallel to the Danube or explains floods by winds blowing at a river's mouth. But he was a pioneer in anthropology and established the four essen-tial criteria of race, language, customs and diet. By this system his accounts of Scythia and North Africa are of the greatest value. He had a good eye for what men eat, and his classification by diet is eminently scientific. He was a keen student of comparative religion and noticed real parallels between Greek and Egyptian rites. He was an observant naturalist, and his account of the crocodile, though not perfectly accurate, is wonderfully vivid and lively. His mathematics were less competent. More than once he makes elementary mistakes, and his efforts at chronology are not uniformly happy. But the fact that he attempted chronology at all shows how far the scientific outlook affected him.

The secret of Herodotus' importance for science is that he collected and arranged a vast amount of material whose importance cannot be overestimated. He preserved in his work all the many subjects which his lively curiosity found. He gives a full picture of what knowledge was available in the fifth century B.C., and his history is a mirror of the age. It has indeed to be read with a critical mind. His account, for instance, of politics in the Persian Wars has to be divested of its heroic colouring before it takes its place in history. We have to discount the tendencious stories of a people who thought nothing of falsifying records to save their name. The miraculous preservation of the Delphic Oracle from the Persians seems to hide a shoddy act of surrender. But modern science has means enough to test the stories and to extract the plain truth from the heroic tale. There remains an invaluable quantity of material, collected and presented with great impartiality. Herodotus had the good sense to record stories which he did not himself believe in case they might be of interest. If he was right to deny the existence of goat-footed men in Central Asia, he was perhaps wrong to be sceptical about the circumnavigation of Africa. But his own judgment is of little importance beside the material. Years of research have shown more and more that for every statement of Herodotus there is usually some justification. He drew on strange sources ; he sometimes misunderstood his informant, but he never invented and he never recorded nonsense.

The matter of his history appeals to many tastes. In a historical guise he preserves stories as old as Homer's. The tyrant who throws his ring into the sea and gets it back again in a fish is of ageless antiquity. The careless young man, Hippoclides, who dances away his marriage, has been traced to an Indian tale whose hero is a peacock. Where Herodotus describes customs, he is usually right. The burial-rites of Scythian kings, the rude form of hockey played in North Africa, the lake-dwellings in Thrace, the use of coracles on the Euphrates, and countless other details are firmly founded on fact. Less probable stories have a basis in reality. The ants " smaller than dogs but larger than foxes " who guard gold in an Indian desert seem to have a real counterpart in marmots on the Tibetan border. The Amazons, placed in Scythia, may be a hairless Asiatic people with matriarchal institutions. The details of offerings brought to Delos indicate the amber-route from the Baltic. The account of the Minoan régime in Crete and its expansion to

Sicily has been amply substantiated by archæology. Even the story of Crœsus being saved from his funeral pyre has the support of Bacchylides.

When we turn to the special problems of Greek history, the position is different. Herodotus' audience knew the main facts, and what he gives is a special version including some succulent details or told from an unexpected angle. This method is tantalizing when he deals with vexed problems of Athenian history, and Herodotus has to be supplemented or corrected by later writers. But when he warms to his task and tells of the battles against Persia, he does something different. He gives the tradition of the great days as it was preserved in different parts of Greece, and if his tale shifts from glorifying the Spartans to glorifying the Athenians, that is because he takes different strands and weaves them into a single story. The epic tone demands a full treatment, and the great events and characters are presented as tradition knew them. It has at times been fashionable to discredit Herodotus' narrative of the war and to reconstruct the battles by the rules of amateur tactics. There are certainly obscurities in his account, but in most cases he himself supplies the remedy, and in others the problem may well be insoluble. In the heat of battle facts are not always accurately noted. What Herodotus preserves is the tradition of the men who fought. He knows

their personalities and the anecdotes attached
to them, from that brother of Æschylus who
clung to a Persian ship at Marathon and lost
his hand, to the Spartan, Deioces, who when
told that the Persian arrows would darken the
sky at Thermopylæ, welcomed it because he
would fight in the shade. Herodotus presents
the saga of endurance and victory, which
came from the fighters themselves, and shapes
it into a heroic tale.

Herodotus is an unrivalled story-teller. He
knows how to vary his tone from the genuinely
grand to the intimate and amusing. He can
tell a breathless detective-story of thieves and
hidden treasure in Egypt or a tale of high
comedy and court intrigue in Lydia. He has
an unfailing eye for the picturesque. Babylon
is captured through a man who gets himself
into the city by cutting off his ears and nose;
revolt in Ionia is started through a message
branded on a slave's head; the messenger who
runs to Sparta with news of the Persian
arrival sees Pan on the way. All is united by
the style. Completely free of archaism or
affectation, limpid, humorous and lively, it is
ideally fitted for narrative. In translation its
beauties disappear, but even then it is impossible not to be amazed by the vitality with
which Herodotus tells his stories or the zest
he brings to the discussion of a theory. A
few words conjure up a landscape or give
the key to a personality. His magnificent
gallery of characters both Greek and bar-

barian is a triumph of portraiture. A single sentence serves as introduction, and the man lives before us.

Behind the art and the science lies the personality of the writer. Of the great writers of the fifth century we know him best in his curiosity, his broad and humane tolerance, his sense of humour and of greatness. We know too his pleasant weaknesses, an occasional gullibility, even vanity. His personality gives the real unity to his work, and its tone is sustained with remarkable art. He was an artist as well as a man. In the enormous world he presents there is not a dull moment. He was, after all, a great historian who cared for all kinds of human activity and possessed the art to make them live. The combination of art and science which he invented and called history has been subjected since his time to many modifications, but he formulated its principles and showed how they could be put into practice. His successors, even the greatest, have only gone farther on the lines he indicated.

The impulse he created found a great follower. Thucydides (471–401 B.C.) was an Athenian of good family, who took part in public life but had the misfortune to be exiled for a naval failure in Thrace. When he was in the prime of life, the internecine war between Athens and Sparta began, and he saw his opportunity for writing history. He survived the capture of Athens by three years, and though he had been long at work, he had not yet finished. In his twenty years of exile he made full use of his time for collecting material and examining witnesses. He was able to visit the scenes of the chief battles and to talk with the protagonists of both sides. He saw and copied important documents, perhaps with the help of Alcibiades. Of the eight books of his history the fifth and eighth show signs of incompleteness and enable us to appreciate his use of raw materials. The first book, setting forth his historical aims and explaining the causes of the war, also shows signs of second thoughts and judgments reconsidered in the light of later events. But the whole work is a masterpiece, perhaps the most satisfactory history ever written.

Thucydides chose the subject of the Peloponnesian War because it was the most notable war yet known to man. He justifies his choice at some length and shows that in this conflict between the naval power of Athens and the land power of Sparta the whole of Greece was engaged on a scale and with resources unprecedented in human memory. He claims that his history will be of use to those who wish " to examine the truth of what happened and of such and similar things which will happen again while human nature remains." His standpoint is that of the scientist demonstrating the truth for the benefit of humanity, and he had a passionate desire to find it. To get it he took the greatest pains, conscious that eye-witnesses contradict one another, that bias and forgetfulness distort the facts. He rigorously excluded the mythical element at the cost of making his history less attractive to some people. For contemporary history he himself examined the witnesses, and when he found it impossible to find the truth, as with the Spartans on military matters, he tells us so. To past events he applied an acute and critical mind. He uses the discovery of tombs on Delos to show that its original inhabitants were Carian and so lays the foundations of archæology. He endeavours to extract truth from legend. For him Minos is the first holder of sea-power, the siege of Troy prompted by the political necessities of Agamemnon's empire. By the comparative study of uncivilized neighbours he was able to reconstruct aspects of past history, and he knew that the Greek claim to be a special race apart was not confirmed by scientific anthropology. For previous historians, even for Herodotus, he had little reverence. He found their chronology inadequate and their treatment meagre. He instituted a proper system of dates based on summers and winters and related to the official posts of Athens and Sparta. No trouble was too great for him, no relevant truth to be shirked. He wrote for posterity and proudly says of his work : " It is composed as a possession for ever rather than as a prize-composition to be heard for the moment.

His story deserves the claims he makes for it. For twenty-eight years with a short intermission the whole resources of Greece were flung into the struggle. The war exhausted Athens and ended that period of human activity which is one of the noblest chapters of the past. The struggle was not merely for territorial or commercial ends. The Athenian and Spartan systems stood for the opposed ideals of democracy and aristocracy and for the ancient antipathy between the Ionian and Dorian branches of the Greek people. In the variety of its events and personalities, in the multiplicity of its issues and the passions which they stirred, the war would in any case arouse great interest. Thucydides treated it as a master, and though he wrote as a contemporary, he saw it with the steady eyes of posterity. From the obscure quarrels in the Adriatic and on the Thracian seaboard to the first temporary and ineffectual peace, then through the titanic and tragic failure of the Athenian expedition to Sicily to the beginnings of the Spartan attack on the Athenian allies in Asia, he guides the complicated story with an unerring, masterful hand.

There is nothing here resembling the broad treatment of Herodotus. Thucydides keeps strictly to the point, and his occasional divagations are either demanded by the narrative or suspicious as notes which he would have rejected from his final text. He deals at greatest length with those episodes which he has been able to verify on the spot or in which he himself played a part. In consequence his narrative has the solidity and verisimilitude of evidence where every word is weighed. Inconsistencies hardly exist, and the whole texture is admirably coherent. He shows too the efficiency of a man who has been himself a soldier and understands the technicalities of tactics and armaments. His accurate and detailed narrative takes note of the weather, the state of the roads, the character of the country fought over, the construction of warships, the fine points of naval manœuvres, the use of military music. No relevant point misses him, and his work is as indispensable to the student of war as to the historian. When he describes complicated campaigns in the mountains of Acarnania and Ætolia or the attempt of the Athenians to blockade Syracuse, his command of the situation leaves no obscurities.

He has too the soldier's excitement in his work. His longer stretches of narrative are enthralling simply because he tells what happens and carries us with him through each stage of success or failure. The account of the Spartan disaster at Pylos, with its unexpected reversals of fortune and the brilliant improvisations of the Athenians, was written by a man who enjoyed the art of war. But the soldier in him is subordinate to the detached observer. He had learned from medicine, the one exact science of his time, and not only does he give an account of the plague at Athens which leaves nothing to be desired in accurate observation, but he treats the whole question of the Athenian failure as a disease whose causes and symptoms can be studied. In particular he watched and analysed the moods and movements of popular psychology, noting its admirations, its fickleness, and its irresponsibility. He understood the mentality of soldiers, and his narrative explains the curious depressions which assailed the opposing armies no less than their sudden exaltation after some successful undertaking.

His greatest triumph is his account of the Athenian expedition to Sicily. It remains unrivalled in historical writing. It shows in perfect combination his intellectual grasp of details, his acute sense of character, his capacity for making a story exciting without any of the resources of superficial rhetoric. He spares nothing from the first wild hopes of the Athenian democracy that it would conquer Sicily, perhaps even Carthage, and the solemn departure of the fleet with libations and prayers, through the indecision of the generals which lost invaluable days and the gradual wasting of the army through disease and battle, to the last fatal fight in the Great Harbour and the final retreat and surrender of the Athenian troops. Treated at considerable length as the ultimate cause of the fall of Athens, the Syracusan expedition seemed to him the culminating episode of the war, and on it he lavished his powers.

The narrative of Thucydides is normally impersonal. He seldom passes judgment on a man or a policy, and he maintains an impartial attitude between the combatants. The effect of detached and intellectual austerity is enhanced by the style. Complicated and difficult, it has none of the easy grace of Herodotus. Even at its simplest it moves through periphrasis and antithesis and shows the influence of the rhetorical sophists, Gorgias and Prodicus. The vocabulary is often unusual and the word-order not the most obvious. But this style is entirely natural to Thucydides. Into it his thoughts fall, and he maintains it throughout his work. Strange at first, it slowly takes hold, and its unfamiliar rhythms stay in the memory until we realize that only in this way could Thucydides have written, and that this style is the right medium for his personality. It conveys the intellectual effort which is the life of his work, and its austere periods are those of a man who set the truth before easiness and simplification. Thucydides had not Herodotus' easy grasp of affairs, and he needed a style suited to his balancing and judicial mind. When we are familiar with it, it has a peculiar eloquence. The sentences are saturated with a powerful personality, and each has its full expressiveness. They have the permanent and satisfactory form of great art.

Occasionally Thucydides breaks the impartiality of his narrative to pass judgment. He was concerned with the lessons of history, but his explicit conclusions are few. The most striking is the disquisition on the civil strife in Corcyra. From a single example he explains the main features of a curse which, sooner or later, affected every Greek state. His statement of its characteristics is as true to-day as when he wrote. It is a study of popular psychology in war, especially civil war, and the main features of hysteria and corruption are sketched with merciless insight and accuracy. More personal are the tributes he pays to the great Athenian statesmen, Themistocles and Pericles. In Themistocles, who died before his own day, he admires the grip on reality and the keen prescience of future events, the right judgment and the quickness of mind. With Pericles he was more concerned as one of the chief figures in the first part of his drama. On his death Thucydides passes what is almost a eulogy on him and praises the wisdom of his policy in comparison with the follies of his successors who deserted it. Other revelations of personal opinion are few. For Cleon, the demagogue who stood for the repression of the Athenian allies and the merciless prosecution of the war, he has a few scornful words, calling him "the most violent of the citizens and by far the most persuasive with the populace at that time."

Thucydides' real thoughts about the war are contained in the speeches he gives to the chief characters at different important turns in the story. To these he relegates those subjective elements which cannot be easily displayed in an impartial narrative, but are indispensable to a proper understanding of events. Through them he explains the motives of the chief actors and illustrates the spiritual and psychological issues at stake. For the speeches he does not claim complete historicity, but he does claim that he " keeps as closely as possible to the general tenor of what was said." They are therefore valuable compositions made out of real historical material, and though the voice is always the voice of Thucydides, the contents come from men who played great parts in the war. There are some forty speeches, and most are of considerable length. The importance which Thucydides attached to them may be seen by their presence in the more polished books and their absence from the unfinished.

For the reader the speeches serve several purposes. They embody the great sayings of the time which passed into popular currency and became part of history. When Pericles says of the Athenians, " We are lovers of beauty without extravagance and lovers of wisdom without effeminacy," he answers the deriders of Athens in ringing words, and when Nicias in his last speech to his defeated troops reminds them that

141

" Men make a city, and not walls or ships
empty of men," he says something that survives imperishably attached to his name.
But most of the speeches illustrate history
in a different way. They give the psychology of the war. At its simplest this is seen
in the great characters who are revealed
through their words. The high idealism of
Pericles, the caution of the Spartan king,
Archidamus, the violence of Cleon clamour-
ing for the whole population of Mytilene to
be put to death, the insolent candour of Alcibiades demanding the conquest of Sicily or
betraying secrets to the enemy, the worthy
and superstitious Nicias trying to instil into
his troops a confidence which he does not
himself share, all these belong to historical
portraiture and are the work of a man who
knew how to delineate men through their
words. Their success explains the absence
of personal judgments from the rest of the
work. Thucydides showed the men as they
were and left his readers to judge.

But the psychology of the war does not
end with that of its great figures, and the
speeches are also concerned with the motives
of peoples and governments. This may be
seen in the events leading to the war which
are illustrated and explained by eight speeches.
The complicated relations between a mother-
city and her colonies, which led to the estrange-
ment of Athens and Corinth, are shown in the
speeches of Corcyrean and Corinthian envoys

at Athens. The Corcyreans claim the right of independent action and ask for an alliance with Athens. The Corinthians answer that it is neither right nor profitable for Athens to grant their request. From this conflict of claims the war began, and Thucydides sets it out with characteristic impartiality. Later follows a full-dress debate at Sparta. The Corinthian envoys make an inflammatory and derisive speech calling for war, and the Athenians answer with a statement of Athenian power and preparedness. The Spartan king, representing the traditional caution of his country, pleads for time, but he is countered by the Ephor who speaks briefly demanding war. The four speeches show the attitudes of the different parties towards war and reveal a cleavage in the Spartan ranks. Two isolated speeches follow to clinch the situation. The Corinthians demonstrate the advantages of war, and in the Athenian assembly Pericles declares his unwillingness to submit to the Spartan demands and emphasizes Athens' capacity to sustain a successful combat. The protagonists have now explained themselves, and the situation is clear. The war can begin.

Most of the crises in the war are treated in the same way, though none on such a scale. By this means the main issues and motives are made admirably clear, and Thucydides shows an unerring judgment when to admit a speech and when not. If the occasion is not sufficiently critical, he records briefly what was said and leaves it at that. His placing of speeches is part of his artistic construction. They mark the movement of events. But they also show what Thucydides felt about the whole story and belong less to science than to art. The story is of the fall of Athens, and through the speeches Thucydides marks the different stages in the collapse. The speech of the Corinthians is practically a eulogy of Athenian brilliance and rapidity of action. The famous Funeral Speech of Pericles is a praise of Athens at her best and noblest, and every sentence of it shows the ideal for which men fought. But Cleon's speech in the Mytilenean debate with its demand for a general slaughter shows a new and nasty spirit, countered for the moment by the good sense of his opponent, Diodotus. But the ruthless temper is not allayed, and in the Melian Controversy Thucydides shows to what lengths false Athenian realism had gone. For political purposes the Athenians offer the Melians a choice between subjection and destruction, and a long dialogue shows the impotence of humane notions against a ruthless lust for power. The Athenians care nothing for the objections advanced to them, and the whole population of Melos is killed or enslaved. Without any explicit statement of his own opinions Thucydides shows the gradual degeneration of Athens from the Periclean ideal.

This artistic attitude may be seen in other aspects of the work and is essential to its structure. The great scale and prominence given to the Sicilian expedition immediately after the Melian atrocities come with the full force of tragic irony. Each blunder in turn seems but a stage in the inevitable defeat of Athens, and when the defeat comes, Thucydides leaves no doubts about its completeness. It was the fatal result of a policy which at the outset he criticizes as alien to Pericles' correct ideas. But it would be wrong to view Thucydides as holding the Sicilian disaster as the punishment for evil done. Any such sentimental notion was impossible for his realistic mind. He had indeed some of Machiavelli's political outlook, and judged a state by its capacity to exist. The successors of Pericles failed to see where the strength of Athens lay, and therefore he condemns them. But he was not a Chauvinist or an advocate of power for power's sake. The Athens he admired was, in his opinion, worthy to rule, and when it lost its power, it had also lost most of its great qualities. But he had no illusions about politics. The good Nicias, with his attachment to omens and divination, was a main cause of the disaster in Sicily, and Thucydides' epitaph on him that he least of all men deserved such a death " because of his complete attachment to conventional virtue " is the verdict of a man who knew that in the destinies of peoples goodness is not enough.

The history of Thucydides satisfies the scientist and the artist. It combines the most careful statement of facts with the form which only an artist can give. It was written by a man used to medicine and capable of transferring his attention to the body politic. But under the dispassionate diagnosis is the strong emotion of a man who knew what Athens had once meant and what a world was lost. He had listened to Pericles, and he must have recorded something akin to his own thought when he made the great statesman say : " The whole earth is the sepulchre of famous men, and not only are they marked by the inscription of monuments in their own country, but even in lands not theirs their memory lives in each man's heart more than on stone."

The history of Thucydides was carried on to the fall of the Theban supremacy in 362 B.C. by a man of different and inferior gifts. Xenophon was a country gentleman, fond of sport and adventure. He admired the Spartan ideal, and found friends in the chivalrous aristocracy of Persia. His voluminous works have survived because, when there was a revival of Attic prose in the second century A.D., he was admired as a stylist and compared to Herodotus and Thucydides. As a historian he has no great merits. An avowed follower of Thucydides, he completely failed to appreciate his master's methods. His work is superficial and biased. He took little trouble to get first-hand material; his history is a panegyric of the Spartan king, Agesilaus; he pointedly ignores the important and interesting Theban general, Epaminondas. He has a conventional standpoint, and ascribes the fall of Spartan supremacy to divine nemesis. He tells moral anecdotes, and Thucydides would have formed a low opinion of his work.

If however his *Hellenica* is disappointing, he atoned for it by his admirable account of his own adventures in the *Anabasis*. This story of Greek mercenaries, marching with a Persian pretender to seize the Persian throne only to have their leader killed in the moment of victory and to be compelled to retreat with enormous difficulty, is a masterpiece of narrative. Its chief merit is its plain adherence to facts which are too exciting to need adornment. As a soldier Xenophon noted all that concerns an army on the march, from the landscape and the cities they passed to the food they ate or the way they crossed rivers or fell into battle-order or argued about the commands given to them. The story is of absorbing interest. This adventure across Asia revealed weaknesses in Persian organization and prepared the way for Alexander's conquests. Written with great ease and fluency, the story never flags; even if it lacks the emotional power of Thucydides, it has some great moments. Cyrus is killed and no one knows it; after months of weary marching in desolate mountainous regions the Greeks at last see the sea.

Xenophon wrote on many other topics. He composed tracts on hunting, the Spartan constitution, and household management. He wrote lives of Hieron and Agesilaus. In the *Cyropædia* he wrote an imaginary and instructive account of the education of the ideal ruler. The book is much too long and soon becomes tedious. Xenophon's political ideas were neither numerous nor profound. But the book has its interest. Xenophon had his ideal of what a man should be. He liked chivalrous and princely qualities, and in his own way he expounds them well. The *Cyropædia* did for the Hellenistic age what Castiglione's *Il Cortegiano* did for the Renaissance. It standardized a tradition and made it the material of education.

Xenophon had been much struck in his youth by the personality of Socrates and devoted books to his memory. His *Memorabilia*, *Apology* and *Symposium* all describe the famous teacher and defend him from the accusations made against him. They have been completely eclipsed by the genius of Plato who dealt with the same topics, but they are not worthless. They show how this man of action saw the influential sophist, and though their historicity may well be questioned, they help to give sides of Socrates' character to which Plato was blind. For Xenophon he is the plain man's philosopher, who solves little conundrums in ethics and economics and can be trusted to give a sensible answer to a difficult question. Xenophon defends him with spirit against the charges of irreligion and corrupting the young, but he has none of Plato's conception of him as a saint. Such a notion lay outside Xenophon's purview. He was an honourable and agreeable man who liked open air and good conversation and good manners. He was in no sense a great man or a genius.

CHAPTER V

OLD AND NEW COMEDY

JUST as tragedy grew from ritual and dances connected with the mysteries of suffering, so comedy grew from rites connected with the mysteries of fertility and procreation. From the earliest times the Greeks had held ceremonies in which ithyphallic processions and rustic ribaldry were combined with cheerful forms of mumming. Such early rites may be seen depicted on vases of the seventh and sixth centuries from Corinth and Sicyon, and tradition connected the origins of comedy with the Peloponnese. But when comedy first appears in a definite form, it belongs entirely to Athens and is, like tragedy, associated with Dionysus. It has become the natural counterpart of the most serious of arts and has for its province mockery and ribaldry. It is performed at fixed festivals ; a prize is given for the best comedy ; its authors are known and quoted. It has become an art, and its origins are forgotten. It found maturity later than tragedy, and its climax was reached in Aristophanes (450–385 B.C.), whose extant eleven plays were all produced after the outbreak of the Peloponnesian War. He is the only comedian from whom any complete plays survive, but he seems to have summed up in himself the main qualities of his predecessors and to be entirely representative of this surprising art.

In construction and manner Greek comedy is far removed from all subsequent comedy. Its form keeps some of the traditional elements. There is the chorus dressed to represent what the poet likes—frogs, birds, old men, women, wasps. It commonly gives its title to the play and is of great importance both for the management of the action and for the expression of the poet's opinions on topical subjects. The chorus-leader has a speech to make in which he is the poet's mouthpiece and talks on morality or poetry or politics or whatever is uppermost in the poet's mind. This is a survival of the old topical joking. The action is varied and vivid, and we find the best and oldest jokes, not excluding those scenes of beating and bullying which lie at the heart of farce. Nor are the ithyphallic origins neglected. Greek comedy is frankly improper, and some of its best jokes are unwelcome on the modern stage. It is also enormously topical. Well-known figures of Athens are made the object of constant ridicule. There is always a debate or dispute in which some important issue is discussed. All these elements belong to tradition ; they are religiously observed and incontinently enjoyed. But Aristophanes combined them

151

into a structure of transcendental farce. The old buffoonery and jesting are but the details of his impossible and magnificent plots and are transferred to a world of pure fancy. He creates fantastically unreal scenes, and peoples them with prominent figures compelled to perform the most ludicrous actions, or he fills a topsy-turvy world with ordinary men and women of his own creation and confronts their plain sense with situations of absurd improbability.

In the hey-day of their greatness the Athenians were willing to have jokes made at their expense and tolerated almost any criticism of their politics and habits. The comedians were allowed to portray public men on the stage without being prosecuted for libel. At times they were thought to go too far, and then they were fined, as Aristophanes was by Cleon, for disgracing the city before the allies and strangers. Aristophanes took full advantage of this liberty for deriding what he did not like and expressing his own views on public policy. With considerable courage and remarkable consistency he kept the same moderate outlook throughout his career and urged his countrymen not to fight Sparta and not to treat their allies as subject tributaries. He drove his points home by making his political opponents as ridiculous as he could make them and by inserting sound pieces of political advice into his work. It says much for the Athenian democracy that it bore his criticism even when it was at war, and at least in the early years of fighting he said exactly what he pleased.

The earliest of his surviving plays, the *Acharnians* (425 B.C.), is a satire on the war-party and the generals. In short and vivid scenes the war is made to look absurd, and without any appeal to pathos its hardships are brought home and shown to be unjustified. Here is the Persian envoy looking "like a man-of-war," the fire-eating general dressing for battle, the starved Megarian selling his daughters as pigs, the public informer sold to Bœotia as a unique Athenian product, the private peace made by the astute hero with the enemy, the undignified collapse of the general while he jumps a ditch and his merciless discomfiture while the hero prepares his peace-celebrations. The whole is taken at a great speed. Scene follows scene and character bustles after character. Crammed with topical allusions and jokes, the dialogue somehow keeps to the point, and each new diversion is complete in itself. All is united by the mockery of war as opposed equally to sanity and enjoyment. But the atmosphere of farce does not prevent us from seeing how much good sense underlies the structure. The causes of war are exposed in a speech which must have seemed admirably true to many hearers, and throughout the poet pleads adroitly for his own cause by making the militarists something less than human. His own sym-

pathies are with his hero, a perfectly sensible
and hard-bitten farmer who with great adroitness faces the problem for himself and solves it.

The *Knights* (424 B.C.) is not written with
such gusto and shows traces of a more bitter
temper. It is an attack on the demagogue
Cleon, for whom Aristophanes shared Thucydides' aversion, and incidentally a tolerant and amused criticism of democracy.
Once again public figures appear on the stage,
this time, the generals, Nicias and Demosthenes, who were later to perish together in
Sicily. But the chief figure is Cleon, the
Paphlagonian hide-seller, who has established
a sinister hold on the old man Demos and
is eventually dispossessed and disgraced
through the plotting of the two slaves,
Nicias and Demosthenes, who replace him by
an offal-seller who is even better at flattery
than he is. The plot is simple, and the play
is more of a bitter satire than a farce. The
action is amusing and the dialogue often
excellent, but the real interest lies in the
treatment of the public personalities. Nicias
is made timorous and respectable, Demosthenes courageous and adventurous but
rather too fond of his drink, Demos slow and
gullible and deeply attached to his little
comforts. Cleon is treated unmercifully. He
is shown to be violent, vain, dishonest, a
receiver of bribes and notoriously revengeful.
Fancy and fact are irretrievably intermingled,
but the characters emerge with admirable

clarity. Their main lineaments must have been true to life, or the poet would not have secured the effect he wanted. His aim was chiefly to discredit Cleon, who stood for a policy and methods of which he profoundly disapproved. He had received hard knocks, and he hit back hard in return.

These two plays are the only cases where Aristophanes presents contemporary political characters on the stage. He followed them by another play, the *Clouds* (423 B.C.), in which he held up to ridicule a figure which has played a greater part in the imagination of posterity than any of the Athenian demagogues or generals. Socrates has been sanctified by Plato, but for Aristophanes he represented all the worst features of the Sophistic Movement, on which the *Clouds* is a brilliant, if rancorous, attack. By contrasting the destructive effects of the new education with an idealized picture of traditional Athenian life he has no difficulty in discrediting the Sophists. Into the character of Socrates he throws all the disagreeable qualities he can find, making him a greedy and dirty old impostor, muttering mumbo-jumbo or proposing preposterous scientific conundrums. His disciples are either lousy students, bent down as if looking for truffles, or unprincipled young blackguards who can prove the worse the better reason and think nothing of beating their fathers. The plot is held together by the relations of an old-fashioned father and a modern son, and its lesson is made clear by the long and partisan argument between the Right and the Wrong Logic. The moral is driven home by the destruction of Socrates' " Thought Factory " at the close.

The contrast between two generations is the theme of the *Wasps* (422 B.C.), though here the rôles are reversed. The characters are all imaginary, and the play is a good-humoured skit on an old Athenian's passion for sitting on juries. The subject is perhaps not sufficient to get the best out of Aristophanes, and the play falls below his usual standard of vitality. There is a good scene where two dogs are tried before the indefatigable juror, and the end of the play is admirably conceived in high revelry. Aristophanes is attempting something more akin to a comedy of manners, but he has not yet found his way to exploiting the characters. Both father and son are well conceived, but without a fanciful setting their peculiarities are not of the greatest interest.

The qualities neglected in the *Wasps* found admirable expression in the *Peace* (421 B.C.) and the *Birds* (414 B.C.). In these two plays Aristophanes gave full play to his adventurous wits and created delicious worlds of fancy. The *Peace* is a political fantasia. An Athenian farmer, tired of war, flies to heaven on a dung-beetle to find that in disgust with men the gods have moved higher and that War is in possession of Olympus and has buried Peace in a cave. The farmer drags Peace out and comes back to earth with her companions Festival and Harvest. He marries Harvest and the play ends with the strains of the wedding-song. In the *Peace* Aristophanes opens new avenues to his talent. The farcical treatment of the gods was well suited to his taste. Hermes as the door-keeper of an empty Olympus and the bullying, blustering War are admirably real, keeping enough of their official character to be convincing creatures of farce.

The *Birds* carries the same principles to confident mastery. Conceived throughout with a poet's fancy, this story of two adventurers who cozen the birds into making an empire in the sky for them is full of extraordinary life and beauty. It may perhaps be a skit on the absurd ambitions which were rife in Athens at the time of the Sicilian Expedition, but the temporary occasion is quite transcended. Scenes of great charm, where the poet reveals an unrivalled appreciation of birds and their ways, are mingled with short skits on familiar types from Athens, and the whole leads up to the superb crisis where the gods, deprived of their empire, treat for terms with the new powers of the air, and the hero marries a goddess called Kingdom. In the *Birds* Aristophanes combined his gifts into a perfect work. The chief characters are admirable adventurers, ready to meet any emergency and always prepared with a repartee. The short scenes succeed each other with great rapidity; not a moment is wasted. The topical jokes have more than their usual brightness when the fat coward, Cleonymus, is depicted as a tree which sheds shields in the winter or Cloudcuckoocity is built by the birds in a way strangely reminiscent of Herodotus' account of Babylon. The same bold fancy brings in Prometheus under an umbrella in case Zeus should see him, and introduces a Triballian god who talks almost unintelligible Greek.

But what gives a peculiar distinction to the *Birds* is the lyrical quality which pervades it and bursts out in irresistible songs. The gift of pure song was already patent in the *Clouds* where the chorus sing of a cloud's activities in limpid and delightful words. It could be seen too in the eloquent defence of the old education, when the young men " rejoice in the season of youth when the plane whispers to the elm." But in the *Birds* it is triumphant. Aristophanes was a real poet of nature who knew how to convey the delight he found in the birds and flowers of Attica. His melodious straightforward songs, whether of the hoopoe summoning the nightingale or the birds telling of their life, are in the true tradition of the great lyric poets. They exalt the whole tone of the play, which ends appropriately to the gay words of a wedding-song.

The renewal of war and the sense of impending failure which hung over Athenian life affected Aristophanes as it affected the great tragedians. True to his principles he refused to acquiesce in a desperate patriotism, and in the *Lysistrata* (411 B.C.) he made a brilliant and outspoken exposition of his opinions. His theme is that the war must be stopped, and he preaches it in a farce, where the women get peace by depriving their husbands of their conjugal rights. Such a subject could not help being bawdy, but Aristophanes' gaiety and ingenuity keep the tone at a level where the bawdiness is purely farcical. His women are brilliant debaters and have a sound political sense. They know the real needs of life and are determined to get them. They stick to their policy and the Spartans come asking for peace, which is settled with delightful hymns to the protecting deities of Athens and Sparta. Though it lacks the lyrical swing of the *Birds*, the *Lysistrata* is a great play, admirably contrived with vivid scenes and real characters. Its moral is proclaimed in plain words, and nowhere does Aristophanes show his political sincerity better than where he asks for a real confederacy of allies instead of a tyrannical empire. Without being in the least solemn he drives his points home.

The *Lysistrata* is Aristophanes' last pronouncement on politics. The psychology of a war-oppressed people did not allow him to continue his lessons, and he may himself have felt that they were useless. Seeking another object for his wit he found it in Euripides. He had already presented Euripides on the stage in the *Acharnians*, but now he devoted the greater part of two plays to him. The *Thesmophoriazusae* (411 B.C.) is a well-constructed farce built on Euripides' treatment of women. The women are determined to revenge themselves on him for the harsh things he has said of them. He sends his secretary disguised as a woman to plead his case, but the disguise is detected and a crisis arises which is solved by Euripides making his own terms with the enemy. Impropriety again plays an important part, and Aristophanes avoids any imputation of unfairness or hypocrisy by justifying many of Euripides' charges against the other sex. The play is written with great good humour, and if some of the characters presented can hardly have been pleased, they could comfort themselves with the absence of rancour and self-righteousness. Even Euripides wins the day, though perhaps not in a way consistent with his dignity.

In the *Frogs* (405 B.C.) Aristophanes breaks new ground and writes a fantasy out of literary criticism. Written immediately after the death of Euripides, the *Frogs* is an attempt to assess his moral and poetical value. Nowhere except in the *Birds* is Aristophanes so emphatically himself. The scene set in Hades, the irreverent treatment of Dionysus, the fresh beauty of the Songs of the Mystics, the superb and apt parodies, the inventiveness which makes corpses sit up and talk or Dionysus dress as Heracles and be afraid of the consequences, show that the last year of the Peloponnesian War found Aristophanes in full possession of his gifts. After admirable scenes of farce the climax is reached in the great scene where Æschylus and Euripides are examined in person to see which is more worthy to be brought back io life. To this comparison Aristophanes brings much more than personal prejudice. His moral prepossessions made him a great admirer of Æschylus, but much of the discussion is purely æsthetic and is the first appearance of literary criticism in Greek. By dint of parody and jokes Aristophanes delivers some good points against Euripides' construction of prologues, elaborated choric style and lack of weight in his iambics. Some good points are also scored off Æschylus, who is accused of bombast and obscurity. Euripides is, of course, worsted, and his defeat is marked by some harsh words at his expense. There was something in his character and influence that riled Aristophanes, who after scoring legitimate points off his art dismisses him as a rogue.

With the *Frogs* the great days of Aristophanes and the Old Comedy ended. The defeat of Athens by Sparta closed the conditions under which Old Comedy was possible. It was too expensive for an impoverished generation, and its outspoken criticism was ill-suited to the broken confidence of a defeated people. Aristophanes survived well into the fourth century and continued to write, but neither the *Women in Parliament* nor *Wealth* has the force and brightness of his earlier work. The *Women in Parliament* is interesting as a skit on the ideas of the equality of sexes and community of property which Plato preached in the *Republic*. Aristophanes may well have read an early draft of the book or have heard its ideas in conversation. But the play lacks vitality. The jokes are beginning to age and there is a lack of dramatic invention. *Wealth* shows a similar lack of spirit, but has an interest because it shows Aristophanes dealing with a subject suited to the time and points forward to the different art of the New Comedy. The plot is an allegory. Wealth from being blind and indiscriminate in the distribution of his favours is made to see, and the good all become rich. The simple idea must have appealed to the penniless Athenians of the day, but it lacks comic and imaginative possibilities. The characters are quite well conceived on familiar Aristophanic lines, but the lack of long choric songs and the jejuneness of the topical references give the play an impoverished air. It is mainly conversation, and there are plenty of moral maxims. It points forward to a new age.

The unique character of the Old Comedy makes it hard to judge its value. It can be compared with no other form of art, least of all with subsequent comedy. In it farce and fantasy are somehow raised to poetry, but it is

impossible to say how far the success was due
to the individual gifts of Aristophanes and not
to the tradition. Its claim is that despite its
topical character, despite the many quips
whose point is irretrievably lost or only eluci-
dated with great effort, it remains amusing
and delightful. Many of the jokes enjoy
perennial youth. Aristophanes was a master
of words, and in his dialogue he uses all the
weapons of comedy, newly coined monstro-
sities, the language of the streets and the
fields, dialect and official language, topical
gibes and bits of old songs. His puns are as
good as puns can be, but his parodies are the
work of genius. The endless transformation
of well-known lines into nonsense or impropriety is only matched by their appropriate-
ness in their new setting. He is a master of
comic bathos who thinks nothing of applying
the most sacred words to improbable and
improper situations. His endless ingenuity
makes his dialogue infinitely sprightly, and
the give and take of wrangling is the breath
of his plays. But in all his creative inventiveness Aristophanes is never anything but
entirely controlled. Everything is managed
with great mastery and economy. No joke
is pressed too far, no list of epithets is too
long. His style, despite its richness, is essentially neat. There is nothing of Rabelais'
endless roll in these dexterous sentences. He
is a master of argument, and attains real force
and power when he expounds his views in that

great anapæstic metre whose movement has been compared to "the gallop of the horses of the sun." Like the tragedians he created a language to suit his needs and varied it till it fitted all his moods and answered all his requirements.

Aristophanes intended to please and his plays have delightfully happy endings. The gods give in to the birds, peace is declared, Socrates is humiliated, Æschylus comes back to life, the good become rich. All that we most want to happen happens. On the way to it absurdities abound. Men grow wings, or ride on beetles to heaven. Every conspiracy succeeds and every dispute leads to someone's complete discomfiture. But the strength of this art is that the characters behave as ordinary people, even if their vigorous slang, their flights of abuse or flattery, of wily dishonesty and wild enthusiasm, make them more vivid and active than in any known life. There is no nonsense about their being better than other men. Even those who propound Aristophanes' own opinions have their moments of admirable roguery when they cheat or bully or yield to the lusts of the flesh. The women provide the proper denial to those who think that women played no part in Greek life. They spar like fishwives and have a fine grasp of their place in nature, but they have common sense on their side which makes the male enthusiasts look silly.

Every comedian and satirist has his serious side and makes his attacks from some principles. Aristophanes could make fun of what he liked, but he also pursued caustically what he hated. A man of conservative temperament and principles, he viewed with distaste and perhaps disgust the alterations which the Sophists produced in Athenian life. He looked back with reverence and not without sentimentality to the great days of Marathon, and his dislike of the new ways was concentrated on two figures, Euripides and Socrates. No doubt much of his criticism was pure fun intended to raise a laugh, and not all his accusations against them need be treated as serious criticism. But he unquestionably disapproved of both and of what they stood for. In Socrates he found a butt for his hatred of a new devitalizing form of education, and in Euripides he tilted at new tendencies in art and music, no less than in morality, which he could not share. But personal dislike must have played a part in his objection to them. They were not to his taste.

On the other hand, he was far from being a bigoted reactionary. In politics he was a man of the centre and he relentlessly opposed the military party. Partly from a real love for the great past, partly from common sense, he preferred the Athens of his youth to any alternative suggested by generals or philosophers. But at the back of his mind lay an overpowering conviction shared neither by Socrates nor by Euripides. He believed in the good life, the life of sense and pleasure and intelligence, and the men against whom he tilted were the protagonists of other ideals. They wanted a neat and rational world or perhaps a world of religious exaltation and puritanical self-denial. Aristophanes was content with the good things of life, and for them he fought unwearyingly against quacks, bullies, boasters, and all those who thought they had the right to interfere with other men's enjoyment.

Aristophanes left no successor in his own art. It ended with, almost before, him. Its place was taken by a genuine comedy of manners which owed much to Euripides in its sentiments and maxims. Middle and New Comedy, as they are called, seem to have been very similar. Their authors, especially Menander (343 ?–293 B.C.), created what we ordinarily mean by comedy, and through the Roman adaptations of Plautus and Terence assisted its rebirth at the Renaissance. Of Menander no complete play survives, but remains found in Egypt and numerous quotations give a good idea of his worth. He wrote for the recreation of a distressed age which did not want to think too closely about itself. His art is an escape into a curious romantic world. He is fond of foundlings and indistinguishable twins, of noble prostitutes and angry fathers. His plays, of course, end happily and virtue is rewarded. Admirable enough in their own day, these ingenious inventions have outlived their freshness, and Menander's plots seem tedious. But he had a charming character and a beautiful and natural style. Easy, tolerant, affectionate, he made his plays repositories of wisdom, especially of that wisdom which makes men kinder and life easier. He is the antithesis of the great men of the Periclean age. He knows that life is a fleeting show, that those whom the gods love die young, that conscience makes cowards of us all. Even St. Paul quotes him when he says that " evil communications corrupt good manners." His proverbs show a grasp of how to live without asking too much of life. They are part of his acceptance of a world where we must not hope for anything more than the possible. He was the best figure his age could produce, but his work cannot suffer comparison with the inspired nonsense and irresistible melody of the Old Comedy.

CHAPTER VI

PLATO AND ARISTOTLE

THE Sophistic Movement, which left such
an impress on Thucydides and Euripides, had
by the end of the fifth century spent its main
force, and reactionary critics claimed that it
was largely responsible for the collapse of
Athens. The enlightened pupils of Socrates
had devoted their talents to the destruction
of their country, and when in 399 B.C. Socrates
was put to death because he " corrupted the
young men and did not worship the city's
gods," there were many honest men who
approved the sentence because they judged
the master by his disciples. But of this judgment time was to bring a singular reversal.
After his death the memory of Socrates was
sanctified by a man of genius, and the pretentious charlatan of Aristophanes was passed
to posterity as a saint. His life and teaching
were the main inspiration of Plato (429–347
B.C.), who built to his memory the first coherent
metaphysic made by man.

In his youth Plato came under the spell of
Socrates, who became for him the teacher who
sought the truth in the right way and was
never deceived by substitutes. The execution

turned this admiration into religious devotion, and thenceforward the master's memory guided Plato's practical and philosophical life. It is almost impossible to say how far Plato's conception of Socrates was correct. It differs equally from that of Aristophanes and from that of Xenophon, but it explains Socrates' hold on his followers and perhaps the aversion felt for him by the average Athenian. Plato's view may be partial, but he cannot be suspected of distorting the truth. He saw a saint where others saw an impostor, and he left the record of his impressions. His conception has far outlived the reality, and influenced posterity as the historical Socrates could never have done. For Plato Socrates represented all that mattered in life, and to this ideal philosopher he pinned his faith, pursuing his course with consistency from youth to advanced old age.

Plato wrote not treatises but dialogues. The form he chose had its origins in the vernacular mimes of Sicily, but its application to philosophy was his own. For thinkers the dialogue had the advantage of presenting several sides of a question and avoiding continuous dogmatism. The several speakers hold different points of view and have a better opportunity of stating their positions than when reported in the abstract language of a third person. For the artist the method had great advantages. It enabled the poet in Plato, repressed from its natural outlet, to find creative satisfaction in the portrayal of scenes and characters. Plato was a born dramatist. The men of his dialogues are real characters, true to themselves and recognizable in their opinions and their way of speaking. There is great art in the way their casual meetings and haphazard talk are turned into philosophical discussion. But Plato was not moved merely by the dramatist's impulse. Socrates had maintained that the best way to find the truth was by the close and continual questioning of other men. He believed neither in dogmatic statement nor in laborious, solitary thought, and when Plato chose to write philosophy in dialogue, he turned the master's method into permanent form. The process of question and answer by which a conclusion is elicited is more vital than any exegesis. We are carried as in conversation from one thought to another, and our experience is widened as it might be in the company of men talking with great concentration and clarity of what lies in their inmost thoughts. By his use of the dialogue Plato avoids the aridity and inhumanity that threatens much abstract thought. The experience he provides never loses touch with life.

Plato's earliest dialogues may well have been written in Socrates' lifetime, and their intention is artistic, almost satirical. He records conversations which had amused him, and is not much concerned with the quest for truth. He liked to see Socrates confounding the self-important and proving to them that they did not understand their business. In the *Ion* he makes genuine comedy from the conversation between Socrates and the rhapsode who regards poetry not as inspiration but as craft, and in the *Greater Hippias* the pretensions of the Sophist who claimed to teach everything in the world are exposed to ridicule by cross-examination. To this period too perhaps belongs a masterpiece, the *Protagoras*, where the drama consists of the conflict between the different conceptions of the good held by Protagoras and Socrates. In the end no agreement or conclusion is reached, and the two antagonists have almost changed places. In these works there is an element of burlesque and exaggeration. The great men are not treated quite fairly, but it does not matter because Plato is concerned mainly with the amusing side of their talk. He is already a master of characterization and description, and he never improved on those opening chapters of the *Protagoras* where young and old gather together before the dawn in their excited anxiety to hear the great thinker who is visiting Athens. Plato's paramount interest was still in the human comedy, and he found his special subject in the play of competing ideas.

The death of Socrates completely altered Plato's art. Thenceforward his work was determined by his desire to justify Socrates to posterity and to develop the implications of his teaching. In consequence his work becomes more definitely instructive and philosophical. It remains dialogue, but its chief interest is not dramatic but intellectual. Through the character of Socrates many important lessons are expounded, and the negative conclusions of the first dialogues are replaced by positive doctrine of great importance and originality. In all the dialogues but the very latest Socrates is the chief character and his views are triumphant. Though great care is taken over the verisimilitude of the historical setting, it is unlikely that the talk recorded is historical. The dialogues show a growth in the recognition of difficulties and a development of ideas which can only be explained by the growth of Plato's own thought. Plato found his own philosophy in that of Socrates and attributed to his teacher views which were the logical outcome of his ideas, even if they were not actually formulated by him. Indeed, it may be doubted whether Socrates had the power or the desire to create a metaphysic, and the philosophy which emerges is not his but Plato's. Plato never put himself by name into his dialogues, and though his abstention was doubtless dictated by a sensitive artistic conscience, it conformed to his view that philosophy can only be found in the discussions of living men. The dramatic setting was essential if argument was to be pursued properly.

The Platonic Socrates is a great character. He is known in more detail than any other figure of the Greek world. His snub nose and protruding eyes, his gait like a waterfowl's, his appearance like that of a Satyr or a Silen, are as familiar as the divine sign which sometimes inhibited his actions, his feats of mystical endurance and detachment, his endless desire to cross-examine all men, his complacent and irritating modesty, his homely and vivid manner of speech, his attachment to the young and his distrust of the great. In Plato's dialogues he conducts the main conversation and is responsible for the constructive thinking. He routs the other speakers with a merciless logic and an eloquent, if unfair, appeal to the ethical emotions. But his real hold on Plato was established by his death. The complete calm and nobility he displayed at his trial and in his last hours sanctified him for his disciple, and the real power of his personality is seen in the four works, *Euthyphro*, *Apology*, *Crito* and *Phædo*, which recount his trial and death.

In each of these Plato depicts the essentially religious and moral character of Socrates and implicitly answers the accusations made against him at the trial. In the *Euthyphro* Socrates is shown really to understand the nature of holiness in contrast to Euthyphro, who has a conventional and muddled view of it. The *Apology* is substantially the speech made by Socrates at his trial, though it must have been polished and altered, as all Greek speeches were, for publication. It explains

what sort of man Socrates really was. Free
from rancour and pettiness, it is sustained by
the conviction that knowledge is the proper
goal of human endeavour and that " a life
without inquiry is not worth living." It is
informed by a simple religious faith, and
Socrates finds death easy, because it brings
liberation from the imprisoning body and
offers the hope of converse with the great dead.
It shows too a man fundamentally proud who,
when asked to suggest an alternative punishment to death, suggests that he be kept in
comfort at the public expense. The man in
his nobility and his irony is revealed in his
last words to the judges : " It is now time to
depart, for me to die and for you to live.
Which of us is going to meet the better lot,
none knows but God."

The *Crito* shows that Socrates was essentially law-abiding, since when it was perfectly
easy for him to escape he refused to do so,
preferring to obey the law, and the *Phædo* is a
record of his last hours and a superb vindica-
tion of his intensely spiritual nature. Written
later than the other three works, the *Phædo*
is on a fuller scale than they are and embodies
more philosophical thought. It consists
largely of a discussion on immortality, and
its shape is too formal, its character too
comprehensive, for it to be a literal record
of what took place. It may, however, be
substantially true, even though Plato was
deterred by illness from being present. It

shows the calm dignity of Socrates in the face
of death and the extreme seriousness with
which he and his friends discuss the problem
of survival. At first they fail to prove the
case for immortality, and a deep gloom falls
on the company, until Socrates revives them
partly by an abstract argument based on the
nature of life, partly by an appeal through
myth to the religious conscience. Then he is
ready to die, and the account of his death
when he drinks the hemlock at sunset and
feels his limbs slowly being numbed is wonderfully simple and touching. We understand
why Plato closes with the words : " Such,
Echecrates, was the end of our companion,
who was, as we should say, of all those of his
time the best and wisest and most righteous
man."

Between the *Apology* and the *Phædo* Plato
composed other dialogues in which he stated
and elaborated characteristic notions of
Socrates. In some of them he is concerned
with problems of ethics. The historical
significance of Socrates lies largely in his
discovery that goodness does not lie in adherence to a written or unwritten code but
in doing what one knows to be right, and in
the *Charmides*, *Laches*, and *Gorgias* Plato
attacks difficulties suggested by this doctrine.
He places the discussions in a time when he
was either not born himself or was only a
young child. They are conducted by Socrates
on equal terms with great men of the Periclean

age and especially with the exclusive and aristocratic circle to which Plato's family belonged. No matter how much he attacked its failures, Plato was deeply drawn to the world of his childhood, and when he placed his dialogues in it, he answered some inborn need in himself which turned away from the confined and impoverished present to a more spacious and confident age. In this company his ideas moved freely, and he could give full rein to his desire for dramatic character-ization.

Behind these three dialogues lies the Socratic paradox that " Virtue is Knowledge," that we would always act rightly if we knew what the right was. This notion is brought out by being contrasted with other conceptions of the good. In the *Charmides* and *Laches* the traditional virtues of moderation and courage are examined and the popular conceptions of them shown to be vague and muddled. In the *Gorgias* the conception that the good lies in " the will to power " is controverted by a statement of the value of the good for its own sake. In each case the method adopted to reach a conclusion is the same. The upholder of the popular or vulgar notion is subjected to a close examination and forced to define exactly what he means. He fails to do so, and Socrates triumphs because he can at least put forward a consistent and tenable alter-native. The drama consists of this interplay between character and character, between idea and idea, and nowhere does Plato display such charm of psychological insight as in these conversations. The natural modesty of boyhood or the mature strength of a distinguished soldier are delightfully contrasted with the restless ethical striving of Socrates. Nor is Plato's presentment of a character distorted if it stands for a wrong view. The champion of " Might is Right " in the *Gorgias* is admirably lively, sensible and charming. Whatever he might think as a philosopher, as a dramatist Plato was still impartial towards his characters.

When not concerned with ethics Socrates busied himself with definition and with what are now the foundations of logic. These interests are set out in the *Cratylus, Euthydemus* and *Meno*. The *Cratylus* is concerned with the relation of names to things and the nature of language, the *Euthydemus* with the ambiguities inherent in speech. Both are gay and lively, full of parody and logical banter. The *Meno* is a more serious affair. It attempts to show that all our knowledge is recollection of something we knew in a previous existence, and it remains a little puzzling. The necessity of denying experience as the foundation of knowledge is forcing Plato out of logic into religious theology. The bounds he has set himself are too narrow, and he is beginning to reach beyond them to vaster and less tangible issues. Indeed, only from the

Cratylus are religious and ethical elements absent. Usually Plato's dramatic impartiality is limited by the shape he gives to the dialogues and the eloquence and emphasis which he bestows on their ethical sections. The end of the *Gorgias* is a passionate appeal to the ethical emotions; the *Euthydemus* is penetrated with the Socratic morality; the knowledge discussed in the *Meno* is essentially knowledge of the good. Behind the satire and the comedy Plato makes his moral purpose increasingly apparent. He can no longer stand outside the struggle. He must follow his master and try to make men better.

This ethical teaching was ultimately based on the religious experience which Plato shared with Socrates. Plato purified and sublimated the simple faith of his master and identified the end of the good man's life with the attainment of absolute truth in a region beyond and outside the sensible world. To this quest for truth he gave the mythology and language of those doctrines attached to Orpheus which saw the body as a tomb and believed in the soul's deliverance from the senses. The *Gorgias* closes with an apocalyptic vision of the life after death, and in both it and the *Phœdo* the traditional symbols of salvation and damnation are held out as more than likely to be true. Though the details vary and Socrates is careful to disclaim any certainty, these visions, described with a mystic's clarity, are essential to the Platonic philosophy.

They convey a picture of man's place as a moral being in the scheme of things, and they are certainly not meant merely to please. These great truths cannot be proved, but at least they cannot be ignored, and Plato's presentation is a direct appeal to the religious consciousness.

Of Plato's private mystical experiences we know nothing, but whether they resembled those of the saint or the mathematician or the poet, they clearly came more and more to dominate his thought and to inspire the two masterpieces of his maturity, the *Symposium* and the *Phædrus*. In these we find the paradox of a complete other-worldliness clothed in the language of sensual joy and bodily delight. The *Symposium* is a discussion of love from all points of view. Six speeches are made in praise of it, and its reality is brought home by the interruption of Alcibiades. The speeches vary greatly in subject and tone. No aspect of love, whether sexual or sentimental or comic or poetical, is neglected, but the climax is reached in the speech of Socrates which makes love the passion for an eternal good, the means for passing from the visible to the knowable world. The passion which seemed entirely earthly is made the main means of liberating the soul. In the *Phædrus* the same idea is developed with great poetical power. Love is the force which frees the soul for its true activities and brings it into touch with the

179

" colourless, shapeless, intangible reality "
which is the only harmonious whole.

To the description of these ecstatic experiences Plato brought the full powers of a prose-poet. In his account of the soul's ascent through particular beautiful things to the absolute beauty, or in his myth of the soul as a charioteer with two horses straining in different directions, Plato writes as a great mystic who uses the imagery of the visible world to convey the glory of the invisible. And yet this rapture and withdrawal, this denigration of the here and now, is combined with his greatest exhibitions of dramatic art and his most delightful presentations of living men. The setting of the *Symposium*, where the great men sit drinking till the dawn and are interrupted by Alcibiades, drunk and excited, full of humorous admiration for Socrates, is equalled only by the opening of the *Phædrus*, where Socrates and Phædrus walk in the country and sit under shady plane-trees by running water while Phædrus reads a juvenile and cynical essay on love. When we read these pages, we see what a poet was lost in Plato and we realize the discord in his character, which cried for a world beyond the senses while it appreciated every sight and sound in nature, which clamoured for an ordered and ethical seclusion, while it enjoyed every variety and aspect of the sensual life.

The discord could not last, and the *Republic*

is Plato's answer to it. In this work of his late maturity the philosopher and theologian triumph over the poet and the man of pleasure. Built on big lines it treats of fundamental questions of politics, and though it begins by being an answer to the Sophist Thrasymachus, who claims that justice is " the interest of the stronger," the answer covers ten books and contains not only a discussion of the ideal state, but Plato's mature conclusions on psychology, art, knowledge, education and life after death. In it the ethical doctrines of Socrates are taken to their logical conclusion and expounded with unparalleled clarity and brilliance. The *Republic* is a discussion of the principles of government, but Plato saw that these principles involved the whole duty of man, and he did not shrink from the issues concerned.

Socrates had complained that politics, unlike other professions, were not entrusted to professionals, but to amateurs, and the *Republic* is an attempt to define the ideal polity and the ideal politician. The answer is that philosophers must become kings and kings philosophers ; then, and not till then, will there be a chance of justice being a reality. Plato sets out this ideal, knowing that it is an ideal, that the state of which he speaks " is laid up in heaven." But to its discussion he brings a precise and even a ruthless mind. Starting from the conviction that power must be combined with justice, he outlines a scheme of education which should produce such a result, and he never shrinks from the conclusions inevitable to his theory. In his determination to abolish private interest he advocates community of women, children and property. In his desire to have the truth taught he restricts the arts, even poetry and music, to severely educational functions. He disclaims the stories of the gods, because God need never change and can never deceive. His ideal ruler is perfectly given to the service of the state because he is at peace with himself and knows that his own good is the same as the state's. His ideal soldier is really brave because he knows how great are the dangers he has to face and yet is ready to face them. Plato is ready to place women on an equality with men, because so far as citizenship is concerned there is no difference between them. He is equally hard on the democracy, in which he lived, and the tyranny, which his childhood's heroes wished to establish. He has laid aside all his romantic and poetical ideas in his anxiety to be perfectly fair, to set out an indisputable ideal of government, to which lawgivers and statesmen must henceforward try to approximate, no matter how impracticable it may seem.

The moral, even puritanical, earnestness of the *Republic* is based on a metaphysical system which still astounds by its completeness and clarity. Plato has renounced the claims of the sensible world and found reality

in the universal objects of knowledge. Only
those who have studied these are fit to rule,
and his guardians are philosophers and mathe-
maticians. The exposition of these metaphysics takes him far beyond the teaching
of Socrates and establishes him as the first
philosophical thinker who found a permanent
reality behind the objects of sensation. No
matter how difficult the point he is making,
he is always brilliantly lucid, choosing the perfectly appropriate example and raising just
the right difficulty. He is no longer a dramatist, but a philosopher. Socrates dominates the
conversation, and the other speakers are finally
reduced to occasional words of assent or
hesitation. So confident is Plato's method
that he can afford to state as dogma conclusions which at the best are based on personal
impression. His comparison of the state to
the individual is justified neither in theory
nor in practice, and his analysis of the different sorts of men appropriate to different
governments, amusing and brilliant as it is,
has nothing to do with political science. His
aim is to convert and to inspire, and when his
material refuses to yield to scientific demonstration, he appeals to the emotions, even to
prejudice and fear. But behind these there
is the passionate conviction that here is something to be done and that it is well worth
doing.

Plato was no mere theorist. He founded
the Academy and, true to his theories, gave

of his best in lectures and personal teaching. Called in 367 B.C. to act as the teacher of the young king of Syracuse, Dionysius II, he went at once and tried in the face of many obstacles to train the young man as the ideal ruler. He failed, partly from the jealousies which infected the Syracusan court, partly from his own uncompromising character. But the experience was of value to him. He set to work to think things out for himself again, to attack the weaknesses he had found in his system. The results were published in the works of his later years. In the *Theætetus, Parmenides* and *Sophist* he approached the fundamental problems of logic. The first shows that knowledge cannot be identified with sensation or with thought. The second is a criticism of the doctrine of universals set out in the *Phædo* and *Republic,* and the third is an attempt to establish categories of being. In these works lies Plato's greatest claim as a logician. In some respects they are difficult and forbidding. A large part of the *Parmenides* is taken up with a complicated discussion of the One, and the different definitions of a Sophist in the dialogue of that name hint at controversies of which we have no knowledge. But though the dramatic element has shrunk and there are no lyrical outbursts, there are moments of great beauty. The account of the philosophic life in the *Theætetus*, irrelevant as it is, is a moving account of the motives and emotions which stirred Plato to forsake contemplation for action. But the real power here lies in the intellectual grip. Nowhere have questions of such intricacy been stated with such ease, or solutions formulated with such claims on our acceptance. Plato was confronted with the task of asking questions never asked before and of creating a vocabulary for a branch of thought which had hitherto hardly existed. By some unreckonable process he surmounted both difficulties with apparent ease.

From logic Plato turned to politics and to religion. In the *Statesman* and the *Laws* he gives his revised views on statesmanship. The first states the theory and the second elaborates the practice. In the *Statesman* he defines the nature of a good ruler and gives full credit to the personal element which he had neglected in the *Republic*. Experience has made him more tolerant in theory, and he even admits that though democracy does the least good of all forms of constitution, it also does the least harm. But if he had become more tolerant of ideas and systems, he had not become more optimistic about human nature. The *Laws*, which occupied his last years and is his longest work, is an attempt to formulate a practicable constitution. Under the fiction of legislating for a new colony in Crete, an Athenian stranger, who may well be Plato himself, assists a Spartan and a Cretan to make a code of laws which represents the ripe fruit of Plato's political thought.

Unlike the *Republic*, the *Laws* is concerned not with an ideal, but with a real world. Plato clearly meant it to be a model for legislators, and some of its provisions were made the practice of the Hellenistic monarchies, Rome, and Byzantium. Though every enactment is based on general principles, fully discussed and clearly enunciated, Plato finds no detail too unimportant. He felt that though human life was not really a serious thing, it must still be treated seriously, and therefore with meticulous care he lays down rules for everything down to the administration of the municipal water-supply and the picking of fruits by wayfarers. Such elaboration was indeed inevitable because Plato did not believe in liberty, and the state he demands must regulate its citizens' lives from birth to death. Babies must be rocked ; between the ages of three and six children will play under the supervision of a committee of state-appointed matrons ; boys must be taken to school at daybreak ; sea-fishing must be forbidden because of its unsettling effects on the character. The educational principles stated in the *Republic* are elaborated to the last detail, and a whole scheme of secondary education is laid down.

An air of defeat and depression hangs over the *Laws*. The great ideas of the *Republic* are regarded as impracticable. Neither wives nor wealth nor children are to be held in common. Even wine is allowed in moderate quantities to certain classes of the community. But the weaknesses of human nature must be curbed. Every man must marry between 30 and 35, and married life must be passed under the public eye. It is unlawful to speak familiarly to a slave or to travel abroad before the age of 40 or to own foreign money. Wealth must be severely limited and the population kept static. The arts must be strictly controlled, because new melodies will destroy the spirit of the constitution. And all is to be kept in order by a hierarchy of magistrates under a Nocturnal Council and enforced by ruthless punishments. Death is the punishment not only for murder, but for embezzlement of public funds, sexual offences, treason, sacrilege, atheism and heresy. If we would see the application of such rules, we must look beyond Byzantium to the Jesuits and perhaps to the Bolsheviks.

Parallel with Plato's interest in politics grew his interest in religion. In the *Statesman* he tells a curious myth of God forsaking the world and allowing it to roll in a course contrary to the right. In the *Laws* he expounds his mature theology and finds the cause of evils in souls corrupted by consorting with folly. In the *Timæus* he provided a cosmology. The work is almost a monologue by a Pythagorean and is a curious combination of science and myth. It contains penetrating discussions on the nature of space, of movement, of time as " the moving image of eternity," of terrestrial and planetary motions. It has too a mythical account of the creation of the world in which a creative theology is mixed with an airy fancy. God made the world out of disorder because he " wished everything to become as like himself as possible," but in the details of the creation Plato allows himself a good deal of humour as he develops the thesis that what is, is because it is best for it to be so. Our heads are round because a sphere is the perfect shape and oysters dwell at the bottom of the sea because they were once the muddiest and thickest of souls. The *Timæus* is certainly mysterious. Its science is too remote for us, its intention too obscure. It is impossible to say how seriously Plato expected us to take it. But under it there lies a great idea. Plato attempts to bridge the Socratic division between reality and appearance by his noble conception of the world as " a visible god, image of the knowable god," and thereby laid the way to a more humane metaphysic.

Plato was one of the most gifted men who ever lived, a thinker of great originality and power, for whom nothing was too difficult and nothing to be shirked, a stylist of incomparable range and charm, a prose-poet and a master of narrative. His influence on posterity has been incalculable. Through the Neo-Platonists and St. Augustine he provided a philosophy for Christianity, and his works sustained the schoolmen in their struggle against Nominalism and Conceptualism. He was rediscovered at the Renaissance, and he is still an inspiration both to philosophers and mystics. On some questions he provided answers which it is almost impossible to reject. But at times it is hard not to feel that his life was a gigantic mistake, that he was deluded into substituting a lifeless mirage for the world of flesh and blood, that his great arguments are based ultimately on the passions and especially on fear. There were indeed unresolved discords in him. He decried the lure of the sensual world, but used its beauties to describe the paradise of his dreams. He decried the great men of the fifth century, but his imaginative life was spent in their company. He attacked the arts with the fury of a great artist and fought poetry with its own choicest weapons.

The truth is that Plato was uneasy in his generation. He looked back to the past and regretted it, but he saw why it had failed, and its failure made him angry. He wished, like the mathematician that he was, to find a permanent solution for the political problem, and he saw it only in the complete reorganization of society. This notion obsessed him and dried up his gaiety and sympathy. He became disillusioned and bitter : he clung more and more to his belief in discipline and punishment. He had none of the high confidence of the Periclean age either in himself or in mankind, and he was the first Greek who was untrue to type. Nietzsche called him "a Christian before Christ," and there is truth in the words. In disgust with the world of appearance he took refuge in abstractions, but they did not content him, and he was forced back to appearances. But in spite of everything he remains a figure of the greatest significance. He has cast a spell on the world, and despite his narrowness and sense of defeat, despite his contradictions and unresolved discords, he remains the last creative genius produced by Athens and his the last voice of an enchanted world already on its way to the dust.

The possibilities of knowledge instituted by Plato were developed and criticized by his pupil, Aristotle (384–322 B.C.). In antiquity his works were admired for their style, but though we possess many books under his name, not one is a piece of literature. All are disjointed notes, taken perhaps at his lectures and full of broken sentences, omissions, grammatical mistakes and obscurities. We can see that the originals must have had their glories, since even in our texts there are moments of wit and even of majesty. But it is impossible to judge Aristotle as a man of letters. He remains, as Dante called him, "the master of those that know." A scientist as much as a metaphysician, he wrote on physics, biology and meteorology. He laid the foundations for the classification of the sciences ; he formulated the rules of logic and created an important system of metaphysics. He wrote with great humanity and wisdom about ethics and started the comparative study of politics and constitutional history. He composed a handbook on rhetoric for the use of incipient orators. In all this enormous activity he never said a foolish thing and he controlled his vast material with the mastery of a gigantic intellect. But for literature this is irrelevant.

Even for literature he did something. In the *Poetics* he wrote the first extant work of literary criticism. The *Poetics* is either mutilated or unfinished and is mainly concerned with tragedy. After the high flights and denunciations of Plato Aristotle seems curiously matter of fact. His aim is to find how the best tragedy can be written, and he attempts to do this by studying masterpieces like *King Œdipus* and *Iphigeneia in Tauris*. His main intention has been abundantly discredited; new masterpieces are not likely to be made by copying old. But in the course of his discussions Aristotle says many acute and wise things. He says that " poetry is a more philosophical and a higher thing than history because poetry tends to express the universal, history the particular," that " through pity and fear " tragedy effects " the purgation of such emotions," that the tragic hero should be one not eminently good nor bad, but like ourselves, whose downfall is due to some error or frailty. Though his method may seem pedantic, he knew a good play when he saw it and deduced his lessons from incontestable masterpieces. His casual remarks are full of taste and insight. He grasped some important points about criticism, knowing that each literary form has its own virtues and limitations, and if he tried to confine tragedy within too narrow limits, he was in the far result justified by the French classical dramatists who followed his every word and wrote masterpieces.

CHAPTER VII

THE ORATORS

THE making of speeches was always congenial to the Greeks. Eloquence was indispensable to the Homeric hero, and Achilles was brought up to be a " speaker of words." The development of democratic institutions enlarged the sphere of oratory, and a public man had to persuade juries and convince the sovereign people. The great politicians won renown for their eloquence and their words were remembered. For Themistocles a few scattered sentences are all that are left, and of Pericles we must judge from the transformed speeches which Thucydides gives him and a few quotations, as when he compared Bœotia in civil war to an oak split by oaken wedges, or in a funeral speech said : " The city has lost its youth : it is as though the year had lost its spring." For the Greeks these great names lay outside the authentic list of orators. Oratory became an art with such special rules that only those who kept them were recognized as models.

The growth of oratory was part of the Sophistic Movement. In their claim to teach the art of politics the Sophists invented and taught theories of public speaking. Aristotle attributed the first of such claims to two Sicilians, Corax and Tisias, who claimed to teach clients how to win cases at law. Their fame was surpassed by another Sicilian, Gorgias of Leontini, who in 427 B.C. came to Athens and made a great impression by his oratory. The single surviving specimen of Gorgias is indeed remarkable. It is full of verbal balance and antithesis, assonance and even rhyme. Elaborated in the extreme, it is hard to follow, and much of it seems intended merely to secure a balance of clauses and parrallelism of words. But it and its like impressed their generation. Gorgias may even have affected Thucydides. He certainly started the history of Attic oratory.

In Athens oratory played a peculiar part. It was not enough for the lawyer and statesman to be a speaker; he must also follow certain rules of construction, and he must have different styles for different occasions. A speech in a court of law consisted of four parts, preface, narrative, proof and epilogue. A political speech usually involved an extra section of invective. The length and balance of the parts was a matter for the greatest care and excited great technical interest. The manner and style of a speech depended greatly on its occasion. A speech in a private lawsuit would be learned by the client and spoken by him. It might therefore be colloquial and simple. A political speech in the

Assembly had to be cast in a grander mould. Grander still were the Epideictic or Exhibition Speeches made at large public gatherings. In these, especially in the Funeral Speeches, a more poetical tone was expected. In consequence each type of speech had its own style and vocabulary. Each manner had to be carefully studied.

Ancient oratory differed from modern in many ways. In the absence of libel-laws contending orators thought nothing of slandering each other with the richest vocabularies of abuse. In the law-courts, where all lay with a jury, pure questions of law were not so important as a good presentation of a case, and we find less attention to precedents than to personalities. Indeed, the tendency was less to point to proved facts than to construct long arguments from probability. This heritage from the Sophists unquestionably led to unjust judgments. It also greatly added to the importance of the orator. A good advocate could get his client acquitted by a judicious and imaginative use of probabilities. It also led to much ratiocination, which now seems tedious. Good evidence was hard to get, and its place had to be taken by argument.

After the great historians and philosophers the world of the orators unquestionably seems squalid. The endless personalities and attribution of low motives show the Greeks at their worst. On the other hand, it is full of drama and local colour. In it we see the

Greeks at home and in business. It has, too, great technical interest. The surviving speeches are for the most part remarkably well written. Great care was taken over the construction and the style. In ages when oratory has been popular, the Greek orators have been copied and admired. They postulate audiences who will listen to long speeches and be swayed by popular emotions. They postulate too an overpowering interest in controversy and a low view of human nature. Granted such conditions, Greek oratory still makes its effect.

The first orator to profit by the new education was Antiphon (c. 480–410 B.C.). In 411 B.C. he played a large part in promoting the overthrow of the democratic system in Athens and in the next year he was executed for treason. Thucydides had a great admiration for his intelligence and praises the speech he made in defence of his life as the best yet made by a man in such a trial. The small bulk of his existing work falls into two sections. One section consists of three Tetralogies or sets of four speeches written as exercises for imaginary cases. They are skeleton-speeches which can be turned to use and they show how early the forms of Greek oratory were standardized. As the professional advocate might plead on either side, speeches for each are given. Only three other speeches of Antiphon survive and all deal with homicide. The most interesting is *On the Murder of Herodes*

written for a Mytilenean who is said to have
killed an Athenian. The defence is both able
and exciting, and in the absence of other
evidence we get the impression that the
accused was innocent. The style is definitely mannered, and the influence of Gorgias
may be seen in the frequent antitheses which
hamper the thought and contribute little to
the argument. But it has at times a concentrated power that recalls Thucydides.

Another public character, from whom
speeches have survived, was Andocides (*c.* 440–
c. 390 B.C.). A man of good family, he became
notorious in the hysterical proceedings which
followed the mutilation of statues of Hermes
in 415 B.C. and led to the recall of Alcibiades
from Sicily. Andocides was thoroughly involved in the scandal and gave information
under promise of impunity. He was, however,
exiled, and his complicity twice caused him
trouble. In 410 B.C. he made a speech, *On
his Return*, trying to get a restoration of his
rights, and in 399 B.C. he had to defend himself in a speech, *On The Mysteries*, from the
charge of taking part in religious rites at
Eleusis when he was disqualified from doing
so. These two speeches are of great interest.
They tell us nearly all we know about a
mysterious and discreditable business. They
also reveal Andocides as a candid and interesting adventurer. In their plain narrative
they recall the events they tell, and their
unadorned style is a better vehicle for such a

story than the elaborate manner of Antiphon. This plainness was deplored by the ancient critics who thought little of Andocides. But for the modern taste it rings true. The man was on trial for his life, and though he was only an amateur, his words are wrung out of him into real eloquence.

His contemporary, Lysias, was a very different character. He was a professional writer of speeches who made little personal contact with public affairs. He was indeed a victim of the Thirty, the tyrants set up by Sparta after the fall of Athens, and he has left a vivid account of his successful attempt to save his life by bribery. But he was primarily an advocate and as such he won the applause of posterity. He writes a style of charming purity and harmony. Indeed, in his own way he is a master of Attic prose, always limpid and always graceful. Without the emphasis of rhetoric he secures his effects and makes the plain telling of a case the occasion for a skilful play on the emotions. In this delightful style his clients were made to speak, and Lysias has a good sense of their characteristics and how to make them appeal to the jury. He understands the right attitude to be adopted by a young and rich man, who may boast in due limits, or by an old cripple accused of getting a pension under false pretences. He takes us into the intimacies of Athenian home-life, and in his speech, *On the Murder of Eratosthenes*, he provides an

admirable melodrama in the lives of simple
men and women. He also wrote for public
occasions, and a *Funeral Speech* survives
attached to his name. Lysias was not an
Athenian citizen and could not give the
speech himself, but he may well have composed
it for another speaker. It illustrates both
his good and his bad qualities. There is the
same surface quality as in his private speeches,
but the emotion is a little hackneyed and the
orator turns back too often to Pericles for
inspiration. The call of a great occasion
was too much for him.

To the same generation belonged Isæus
(*c.* 420–*c.* 350 B.C.), whose eleven surviving
speeches are all concerned with wills and cases
of disputed inheritance. He was a specialist
who understood an extremely difficult branch
of Athenian law, complicated by intricate
rules of consanguinity and the ignorance of
juries. Isæus was able to expound these
difficulties and to win his cases by the clarity
he brought to the issue. In his speech, *On
the Estate of Hagnias*, twenty-three members
of a family are mentioned, and it is not perhaps surprising that a wrong verdict was
given. Isæus has no great merits as a writer
and his place is more in the history of law
than of literature. Like Lysias he uses the
current vocabulary. At times he condescends
to a conversational phrase or a rough metaphor, and at times his grammar seems to be
at fault. But on the whole he knew his

business well, and he is not to be blamed if he repeats a point or ends a speech with a recapitulation of points instead of an appeal to the emotions. He makes no attempt to accommodate his speeches to his clients' characters and relies on the power and force of his arguments. He is, in fact, not an orator, but a pleader.

Of far more ability and influence was a man who was not strictly a speaker at all. Isocrates (436–338 B.C.) was born before the outbreak of the Peloponnesian War and lived to see the triumph of the new power of Macedon at Chæronea. He came to win a great political influence, and he had relations with most of the great men of his time. He practised oratory as a young man, but lack of voice and nervousness hampered him and he gave up practice for instruction. As a teacher he was unrivalled, and when a competition in eloquence was held by Artemisia of Caria in memory of her husband, all the competitors were pupils of Isocrates. He published works in the form of speeches, and therefore he was counted an orator, but his real contribution to oratory lay in other directions.

Isocrates had strong views on style which he exemplified in his own works and instilled into his pupils. He aimed at producing an exalted effect, and for this he devised technical means. He advocated the avoidance of hiatus between words, that is of allowing a word ending with a vowel to be followed by a word beginning with a vowel. He proscribed certain combinations of consonants and the repetition of the same syllable in consecutive words. He paid great attention to rhythm and maintained that oratorical prose has rhythms of its own. His sentences are built into great periods and he hardly ever allows the variety provided by short sentences. The result is that his style, though admirably careful and indeed faultless, lacks colour and tends to become monotonous. But his ideals drilled his pupils in a strict school and purified the language of Greek rhetoric.

Isocrates had a great influence on the thought of his generation. His writings are often concerned with education and the practice of politics. To both he brought a broad outlook and an admirably consistent point of view. In his tract, *Against the Sophists*, he laid bare the vice of the Sophistic training by showing that its preposterous promises undermined industry, and its claim to teach truth was entirely disingenuous. His constructive theory appears in *On the Antidosis*. There he claims that " philosophy is for the soul what gymnastic is for the body," and he advocates the importance of culture. His view of education is practical, almost philistine. His philosophy is a useful training for life, not a life devoted to the search for truth. But like Plato he was concerned to produce good citizens, and he seems to have been a conscientious and thorough instructor.

His theories of education were based on a political ideal. He saw, as did few of his contemporaries, the immense importance of the new Macedonian monarchy. He realized that Philip was capable of uniting Greece as no city-state was capable, and on this he based great hopes. In the endless quarrels and wars of the Greek cities he saw not only a danger to Greek civilization, but the main cause of the survival of Persia. He wanted the Greeks to unite against Persia, and in his *Panegyricus* he called on Philip to assume the task. With an insight that must have seemed ridiculous to many of his contemporaries he pointed out the weakness of the Persian Empire, and his suggestions for its subjugation, especially by the foundation of Greek cities in Asia, were actually followed when Alexander set out to found his world-empire. Isocrates may have overrated Philip's goodwill, but in his general policy he anticipated what was to come with a clearness denied to most men of his time.

In circles where detachment was less serene, the growth of the Macedonian monarchy caused very different feelings. The right policy to be adopted towards Philip was the main problem for the practical and political orators of the fourth century. It excited the greatest animosities and created lifelong feuds. His supporters were accused of corruption and treachery, and his opponents claimed for themselves the monopoly of patriotism and honour. The issues were indeed confused, and even now it is hard to apportion praise and blame. It is easy to convict the Athenian patriots of short-sighted provincialism. The cause of Philip and Alexander triumphed ; the city-state was doomed ; and the great Hellenistic kingdoms took its place. The small purview of Athens seems negligible in comparison with Alexander's empire stretching from the Danube to the Hindu Kush. On the other hand, the Athenian patriots fought for something of inestimable value to the world. Even the diminished Athens of the fourth century was a greater nurse of civilized life than the diluted Hellenism which the Macedonian armies carried across Asia, and for Athens herself the triumph of Philip meant more than the loss of political independence. It meant a long period of hardships from competing war-lords until all was obliterated in the triumph of Rome.

The controversies of these hectic years brought Greek oratory to its classical form. In the patriotic speeches of Lycurgus (c. 389–324 B.C.) Isocratean principles were put into practice, though not for a Pan-Hellenic end. An unbending and uncorrupted patriot of the old school, he was opposed to any compromise with Macedon and relentlessly pursued any Athenian who could be suspected of treachery. His only surviving speech, *Against Leocrates*, is for the prosecution of a man who ran away after the defeat of Chæronea and justifies the ancient verdict that Lycurgus dipped "his pen not in ink but in death." The poor runaway is assailed with quotations from Tyrtæus and Homer, and his acquittal is regarded as tantamount to the betrayal of Athens, her religion, and her ships. The safety of the commonwealth must come before mercy. Leocrates was acquitted by one vote, so great was Lycurgus' appeal to patriotic sentiment. Perhaps the jurymen were stirred by his hyperboles and felt moved when he said: "So imagine, Athenians, that the land and its trees are supplicating you : that the harbours, the dockyards, and the walls of the city are imploring you : that the temples and holy places are urging you to come to their help." He knew that he was addressing men who would not be shocked by a little exaggeration.

His contemporary and political ally, Hyperides (389–322 B.C.), is known only from fragments. He was an unremitting opponent of Macedon and his policy even forced him to prosecute Demosthenes and get him exiled. The best preserved of his works are a speech, *Against Athenogenes*, and a *Funeral Speech*. The first concerns a foolish young man who has been duped into taking on a business encumbered with debt and tries to get out of it. It is composed in an admirably easy style, not unlike that of Lysias. The *Funeral Speech* is more formal and mannered, but because it commemorates the speaker's friend

Leosthenes, it has a warmth uncommon in such compositions. The noblest passage is that where he offers an unusual consolation to the kin of the fallen by telling them that " if the dead have consciousness, and are under the care of God as we believe, we may be sure that they, who upheld the honour of the gods when it was threatened, are now the objects of God's loving-kindness."

The style of Hyperides was praised in antiquity and he was thought " the best of all who are not specialists." He had many ways of diversifying his style. He used colloquialisms that suggest the Old Comedy; he tried bold metaphors and even elaborate similes; he took great pains with his composition, and in his *Funeral Speech* followed Isocrates' rules for avoiding hiatus. He knew how to combine long and short sentences; he was a master of sarcasm and he was renowned for his wit. His view of his work and his opponents may be seen in his words: " Orators are like snakes; all snakes are equally loathed, but some of them, the vipers, injure men, while the big snakes eat the vipers."

The representative figures of this oratorical world were, however, two men who opposed each other all through their careers and of whose oratorical battles complete speeches survive. Demosthenes (384–323 B.C.) and Æschines (390–c. 325 B.C.) concentrate in themselves the angry and ungenerous passions of these hectic years. They were politicians as well as pleaders, and their speeches influenced the course of events. If Demosthenes pursued a single policy with consistency, Æschines was the perfect opponent who hid his lack of political aims under a biting tongue and a mastery of legal technicalities. The two men were contrasted in their origins, their characteristics and their destinies. Æschines was a man of humble and impoverished family who fought his way forward by force of will, a commanding presence, and a ready gift of speech. His policy of political opportunism never excited overwhelming animosity, and he seems to have died comfortably as a teacher of rhetoric at Rhodes. Demosthenes came of a rich family, but his guardians squandered his patrimony, and his first speeches are those in which he seeks restitution from them. His political life was devoted to the single end of opposing the power of Macedon. At first unsuccessful, he came later to power and was largely responsible for the successful conduct of Athenian affairs between 340 and 338 B.C. He came into violent conflict with his own patriotic colleagues and was exiled at the instigation of Hyperides on a charge of bribery. He returned later as a hero and committed suicide rather than submit to the Macedonian general, Antipater.

Demosthenes became an orator by the force of circumstances and his own political ambitions. He was not naturally gifted, but he overcame his disabilities by hard work and assiduous practice. Even so he was never a ready speaker, and there was probably truth in the claim that his work smacked of preparation. Æschines gives an amusing and plausible account of his complete breakdown on an embassy to Philip, when Philip gave him every opportunity to continue and he remained tongue-tied. But it was precisely this natural difficulty that made Demosthenes a great speaker. Because of it he studied his art with great concentration and polished his speeches until there was nothing imperfect left in them. He could not afford to hesitate and rely on improvisation. Everything was prepared and considered. Therefore his speeches are classics. Granted the occasions they served and the personality of their author, they could not be better than they are.

His speeches fall into three classes : those delivered in private cases in the law-courts, those delivered in public cases, and those made in the assembly. The first are legal, the second half legal and half political, the third entirely political. The private speeches are on the whole short and simple. Their chief interest lies in the life they reveal. Here is a dispute between neighbours which turns on whether a road is a watercourse ; a quarrel begins in camp and is carried on later till the prosecutor is left senseless on the road ; a man claims that he is really an Athenian citizen but has had his name maliciously removed from the roll; a chief clerk inherits a banking business and is defended against the financial claims of the former owner's son. The speeches were not delivered by Demosthenes himself, but by his clients. He was a professional who did his best for money. It is therefore not surprising to find him first writing a speech, *For Phormio,* and then another speech, *Against Stephanus,* who had been a witness for Phormio and was accused of perjury.

The art of the private speeches is interesting. They are written suitably for those who have to deliver them, and lack the polish and display of the public speeches. If their jokes are rare and unconvincing, they have still some admirable qualities. Demosthenes knows how to make the best of a case by appealing to ethical prejudice or to arguments from " probability." His statement of legal points may not be impartial, but it is well suited to the mentality of his juries. The nearest approach to literature may be seen in the passages of narrative which have the simplicity of Lysias. Demosthenes is a master of story-telling and knows exactly how to engage the jury's sympathy by an apt and well-chosen narrative. Without passing too many hostile judgments, he secures through a good story just the right degree of prejudice in his hearers.

His public speeches are of a very different character. Here he acted not professionally, but from his own overpowering convictions.

In seven speeches delivered between 351 and 341 B.C. Demosthenes showed perhaps his greatest power as an orator. The *Philippics* and *Olynthiacs*, the speeches *On the Peace* and *On the Chersonnese* have a single object, the hindrance of Macedon. In them Demosthenes attempts first to awaken his countrymen to the deadly significance of Philip's progress, and then to propose measures to counteract it. His measures were practical and sensible. He advocated an efficient expeditionary force, the conversion of the Festival Fund into a War Fund, active and immediate interference with Macedonian aggression. His method of putting these ideas forward is impressive and persuasive. Avoiding recriminations and personalities, he concentrates on the main point and hardly leaves it. Each speech hammers at a single danger and the means of combating it. His difficulty was to persuade his audience of the seriousness of the situation, and when events put that beyond question, he was faced with the opposite difficulty of persuading them that all was not yet lost. In both cases he kept his temper and his dignity.

These speeches are the most satisfactory left by Demosthenes. They are infused throughout by a patriotism beyond question. Demosthenes contrasts the humiliating present with the great past and hopes that something may be done to redeem the name of Athens. This theme constantly recurs and is the clue to Demosthenes' politics. He had a real appreciation of the Athenian achievement and was anxious to preserve it for the world. On the other hand, he saw in Philip much more than the enemy. Appalled by his activity and disregard for the conventions of war, he saw in him a barbarian who combined a disreputable private life with the deliberate corruption of public issues. His honesty in his disapproval is beyond question, and he seems never to have asked how a man of such low character could do what Philip did. For his own solutions he claimed no special virtue, and he meant what he said when he closed the *Third Philippic* with : " If anybody can offer anything better, let him name it, and press it : and whatever you decide, I pray to heaven it may be for the best."

The reputation of Demosthenes rests not so much on these speeches as on those which he made in public cases before the law-courts. The speeches, *Against Androtion, Against Leptines, Against Timocrates, Against Aristocrates* and *Against Midias*, are composed on a far larger scale and show other sides of his personality and art. They are concerned with the prosecution of men who have made proposals or committed actions which involved public consequences. In most of them political issues are involved, and Demosthenes discusses them with much more violence than in his public speeches. The most characteristic is the speech *Against Midias*. Midias was a political and personal opponent who

eventually slapped Demosthenes in the face
during a public performance in the theatre.
Midias might theoretically be severely pun-
ished for sacrilege, and the speech against
him is an extraordinary piece of work. Demosthenes treats the insult with unparalleled
seriousness and accumulates a long account
of Midias' previous misdoings. Pathos and
humour, anger and self-pity, are called in to
denounce the wrongdoer, and the result is
that Demosthenes soon loses our support.
He asks for too much sympathy and indignation. Nor is it surprising to learn that the
case was compromised and Demosthenes accepted half a talent as compensation. It
looks as if his injuries were not so serious as he
thought them, and he was stressing his case
from political or personal motives.

The climax of this style is to be seen in
the two speeches, *On the Embassy* and *On the
Crown*, which arose from the hostility of
Demosthenes and Æschines. The quarrel
was of old standing. In 348 B.C. Æschines
had taken part in the peace negotiations with
Philip, and Demosthenes prosecuted him for
taking bribes. Æschines countered with an
attack on Demosthenes' associate, Timarchus,
whom he accused of an immoral life, and won
his case. In 343 B.C. the same issue came to
the front again ; Demosthenes made his great
speech *On the Embassy*, and Æschines replied
with a speech known under the same name.
Demosthenes was in a difficult position.

There was no evidence that Æschines had received bribes or betrayed Athens. On the other hand, he had undoubtedly made promises and speeches which led to the occupation of Thermopylæ by Philip and to the ruin of Phocis. The question was whether he was a fool or a knave. Demosthenes tries to establish the second alternative by describing his career. The speech is curiously arranged, and the different events are not always easily distinguishable. This is probably deliberate, as in the absence of direct evidence Demosthenes resorted to proofs from probability and relied on general statements to confuse and convince the jury. Æschines replied with a brilliant speech which derides Demosthenes and proclaims his own innocence with the excuse that he was tricked by Philip. He was acquitted.

In 330 B.C., after Alexander's departure for Asia, Ctesiphon proposed that Demosthenes should be rewarded with a gold crown for his services to the state. Æschines in his *Against Ctesiphon* spoke against the proposal on the grounds that it was illegal, and Demosthenes answered with his most famous speech, *On the Crown*. The occasion provided each speaker with an opportunity for reviving old disputes and discussing his own and the other's political past. Æschines makes his claim on sound legal grounds, but foolishly proceeds to discuss the past actions of Demosthenes. He recapitulates occasions, sometimes trivial, when Demosthenes' policy has not been to his country's advantage. Demosthenes answered with his own version of the events and a counter-attack on Æschines as a low-born traitor. Assuming that his and the city's thoughts are one, he finds it easy to discredit his opponent. Æschines lost the case and was condemned to a fine. Rather than pay he retired into exile.

In these great contests the characters and oratorical methods of the two men are shown in sharp relief. It is easy to take sides and to belittle one of the antagonists at the expense of the other. But it must be admitted that they were well matched and that each gave as good as he received. Demosthenes has the advantage of having pursued a plainly patriotic policy and of being able to prove it. Æschines claims for himself that "both individual and state must shift their ground according to change of circumstances and aim at what is best for the time." His defence of his own actions is not entirely satisfactory, and it is just possible that from conviction or corruption he wanted the triumph of Macedon. Naturally he could not tell such a truth before an Athenian jury, and he had to confine himself to vague patriotic sentiments and accusations of failure against his opponent. This difference between their positions accounts for the best passages in Demosthenes. His eloquence rises to its highest when he describes the stirring events of the previous years or expounds his deepest hopes for Athens.

On the human side, however, the scales are more evenly balanced. Demosthenes' humour is awkward and his attacks on Æschines' humble education almost ludicrous. It is hard to believe that they were treated seriously. Though he varies his style and his sentences, he does not really vary his tone. Every point is made with the same violence, every sentence is underlined. His strict control of an emphatic rhythm makes lightness of any kind almost an impossibility for him. Even his great metaphors could be turned to ridicule and were omitted from the revised versions of his speeches. On the other hand, Æschines was a natural orator who felt the pulse of his audience and knew how to vary his mood and tone. His jokes and plays upon words are successful. He has a real sense of comedy, and his account of Demosthenes' collapse before Philip is admirably entertaining. He has a pleasant vein of sarcasm and an agreeable way of criticizing Demosthenes as if he were an acknowledged blackguard. His account of Demosthenes' lying leaves nothing to be desired : " When other impostors tell a lie, they try to speak vaguely and indefinitely, for fear of being convicted of falsehood ; but when Demosthenes tries to impose upon you, he first of all enforces his lies with an oath, invoking everlasting ruin on himself ; then, though he knows that a thing can never happen at all, he dares to speak with a nice calculation of the day when it is going to happen." When he attacks Demosthenes' family life, he avoids excessive exaggeration, and his hits are sometimes not far from the truth.

It seems too that Æschines made the utmost of the opportunities which his difficult position afforded him. He based his position on legality and left the appeal to passions largely to his opponent. His adroitness and dexterity are a pleasure to watch. His weakness is that if he ever had a policy he cannot disclose it, and that when it comes to a competition in patriotism, he is inevitably worsted. If there is little to choose between the two in the questions of distorted facts and falsified evidence, Demosthenes has the unquestionable advantage when it comes to politics, not merely because he can claim to have maintained a consistent policy, but because his peculiar kind of eloquence is well suited to the angry and violent passions which politics arouse. By accusations of treachery and threats of ruin he establishes his claim to patriotism, and at least in the speech *On the Crown* he carried the jury with him.

In later antiquity Demosthenes enjoyed an unparalleled reputation. In the Hellenistic world and later at Rome he was the archetype of a great speaker. If at times he seems exaggerated, it is because we have lost the habit of listening to long speeches. It is therefore hard to judge him as a man, or his work as literature. His opinions seem too violent to be altogether sincere, and yet there is no question of his ultimate honesty. His style seems too mannered to carry an audience away, and yet there is no doubt of his success. The complicated form and elaborate periods may delight the student, but it is strange that they should have charmed juries. The fact remains that the Greeks were peculiarly susceptible to rhetoric, and gave it the same undivided attention which they gave to tragedy. Demosthenes swept them away by the power of his emotional appeal and the apparent cogency of his arguments. The qualities we may find repulsive, his narrowness, arrogance, lack of humour and lack of taste, only contributed to the general impression of sincerity and power. This was a man who knew how to persuade.

CHAPTER VIII

ALEXANDRIA AND AFTER

THE fall of Athens meant the end of popular art in Greece. The epic, the choral ode, comedy and tragedy, even the history of Herodotus, had been performed at public occasions and enjoyed by crowds. But the fateful changes of the fourth century ended all this. The Greek world was partitioned between military monarchies, and Greek civilization was carried to the Indus by Alexander and maintained by his successors in the half-Asiatic kingdoms of Egypt, Syria and Pergamum. Autocracy took the place of democracy, even of aristocracy. Art and literature became the privilege of a few. Scholarship came into existence, and scholars wrote poetry as scholars will. Deprived of its traditions, transported to alien climates, patronized and hampered by despotism, literature never again touched its early summits. But even in this restricted sphere the Greek genius still found new things to say and new ways of saying them.

The fourth century was an age of prose. Plato began his career as a poet of unexampled promise, but philosophy stifled a gift that

217

might have equalled that of Simonides. Some thirty elegiac epigrams survive under his name, and among them are some of the most beautiful short poems in the world. Writing with effortless ease on simple themes like the passing of time or shipwrecked sailors or Athenian dead in Persian soil, he manages always to record some exquisite or pathetic moment. At its best his simplicity challenges Simonides, and though he lacks the older poet's majesty, he has the same art of making his rhythm rise and fall in exact harmony with his emotion. He has too a wonderful fancy, which turns a pretty trope into a high flight of the imagination. Without preparation he gives just the moment that matters to him, just the imagery that suits it. The result is pure essence of poetry. As untranslatable as Simonides, once at least his echoes have been caught. Shelley gives the spirit and almost the cadence of an epigram.

> Thou wert the Morning Star among the living
>   Ere thy fair light had fled;
> Now, having died, thou art as Hesperus giving
>   New splendour to the dead.

But Plato abandoned poetry, and the fourth century remained true to philosophy and oratory. Poetry revived in the third century when the centre of Greek life had shifted to Alexandria. There under the benevolent Ptolemies a small circle of gifted men wrote verses for each other. Cut off from active life, they lived only for letters, and their work lacks the range and depth of the great days. But because of their sincerity and their technical accomplishment the Alexandrians have their place. They broke new ground. They were the fathers of romanticism, of learned poetry, and of that poetry which concerns the everyday feelings of civilized men. They created the pastoral idyll and the literary epic. They did much for love poetry. They exploited the unexpected and the recondite. In their own way they showed a strong creative impulse, even though circumstances were opposed to its full satisfaction.

The chief figure of the movement, though not its best poet, was Callimachus (310–c. 240 B.C.). He presided over the arts, and thundered against those who would not accept his canons. He thought, not without reason, that the age of great art was over, that long books had become a bore. He himself wrote hymns and epigrams, and his longer works were collections of disparate episodes loosely connected together. His aim was to startle and amuse. He lacked lilt and swing, but he had wit and neatness. His sterility made him difficult and complicated. His learning helped him to obsolete words, and he enjoyed distorting the natural order of a sentence. His emotions were limited, and perhaps the liveliest were the malice and contempt excited in him by his rivals. He saw himself as the piping grasshopper, and he made few attempts to override his natural limitations. He is at times indescribably tedious, especially when he wishes to impress by his knowledge of geography or mythology. But he has some genuine gifts. His epigrams are often graceful and even touching. He had studied the old masters with profit, and recovered some of their simplicity and directness. In them he abandons his illiberal rancour and writes with delicate affection of those he loves. But his chief gift is romantic. He knows how to create an atmosphere of supernatural tension. He depicts in trembling words the deathly noonday silence on Helicon before Teiresias sees Athena at her bath, or the excitement at Apollo's shrine before the god's epiphany, when the sacred palm-tree trembles and the gates open of their own accord. It is here rather than in his more arid or realistic moments that the poet in him overcomes the professor, and he adds something new to imaginative experience.

Callimachus thought little of his contemporary Apollonius of Rhodes (295–215 B.C.). He disliked the revival of the epic to which Apollonius devoted his talents, but for all its mannerisms and affectations the *Argonautica* is better poetry than anything written by Callimachus. Apollonius chose for his subject the age-old story of the Golden Fleece, and attempted to write an epic in Homer's language and Homer's metre. The result is curious. Of genuinely epic tone there are few traces. The hero, Jason, is uninteresting when he is not repellent. His companions, though properly dressed for the occasion, have none of the heroic vitality. The narrative is a string of episodes and has no architectonic unity. In the first two books it looks as if the story will never get started, so laborious is the mythology and so detailed the account of every action. Apollonius was deeply imbued with the Alexandrian spirit, and thought that erudition and prettiness were adequate substitutes for inspiration and beauty. He devotes many lines to a catalogue of the Argonauts or to Eros playing knuckle-bones with Aphrodite. But in the last two books he finds his real gifts and creates a new form of poetry, the poetry of romantic love. In the love of the young Colchian girl, Medea, for the adventurer, Jason, he has written something of unique beauty. With perfect sympathy he recounts this passion from the dream which tells Medea of Jason's coming to the terrible scenes where he tries to desert her after all she has done for him. The details were borrowed by Virgil in his account of Dido's love for Æneas, but Dido is a mature woman and Medea a mere girl. She has the freshness of a young Colchian princess ; her magic is part of her wildness, and her love is purely romantic. For Jason she betrays her parents and then is ashamed of it, but when she sees him again, she feels that he is like Sirius rising out of the Ocean, and so great is her desire for him that she cannot speak nor move.

At the same time other gifts of Apollonius are brought into play, and the account of the trials undergone by Jason is a masterpiece of mysterious and thrilling narrative. The climax is reached in the sinister lines where he sows the dragon's teeth, and from the ploughland the crop of bronze-armoured men grows as bright as the stars after a snow-storm on a winter's night. In scenes like this Apollonius creates a true romantic art. But he has another gift. He recognizes the beauty of little things, and though at times he falls into mere prettiness, he can also create scenes of delicate charm, when the nymph draws Hylas down into her pool, putting her arm round his neck, or when Thetis and her sea-nymphs carry the Argo through the moving rocks as girls play at ball on the seashore. The *Argonautica* is rich in fine observation, and Apollonius had an eye for undiscovered graces. His genius indeed is limited, and he has few epic qualities, but he was a pioneer of romance and the inventor of love at the end of the world. He was right not to compete with Homer in heroic saga, and when he wrote of what he understood instead of trying to be fashionable, he produced something of true tenderness and beauty.

The third poet of Alexandria, Theocritus (*c.* 316–*c.* 260 B.C.), was greater than either

Callimachus or Apollonius and had a vast influence on posterity. He wrote Idylls or " pictures," and his main theme was pastoral life in Sicily. Attempts have been made to interpret these scenes as the record of the poet's converse with his fellows, and there may be truth in the notion. But for us they must be taken at their face value as poems about Sicilian shepherds, and if they are so taken, they are perfectly satisfactory and complete. Theocritus' world is of the purest fancy, but such is its beauty that it is always alive and real. The shepherds are not yokels but poets, their songs the record of an impossibly delightful life. This is a world of pure art, where everything is harmonized by the imagination and fitted into a complete and entrancing unity.

None of the Idylls are long, and each is complete in itself. Theocritus concentrates his powers and brings off his effects in a small compass. The themes have become familiar through the countless imitations of pastoral poetry, and they are the eternal themes of song and counter-song, of love and death. But whereas in his imitators these themes are standardized, in Theocritus they have a perfect freshness. The settings are chosen by a man who loved nature, and the whispering pine-tree, the caves with clustering vines, the shady halting-place by the roadside, are chosen with faultless tact and taste. No action is dulled by convention. The preliminaries and the prize-givings are equally detailed and lively. But the essential power of Theocritus lies in his capacity for conveying one subtle pleasure after another simply by his collocation of words. He knew that on this small scale every word must tell, that there must be none of the easy repetitions of the epic or the conventional aids of the drama. Every sentence tries to please, and succeeds. Theocritus is full of surprises, and never lapses into a stock form of words or even into a familiar combination of adjectives. He writes normally in the Doric dialect of Sicily, but his style has few traces of " native woodnotes wild." The rustic colouring is put on by a man who knows how to use it for his own purposes and is no pedant in his treatment of it.

The pastoral world, which Theocritus created, remains, in spite of innumerable imitations, a world of eternal charm. In this cloudless landscape the characters live at the level of lyrical joy and sorrow. There is the lover threatening to throw himself into the sea, the poor boy who hangs himself, Polyphemus pining with love for Galatea, the girl Bombyca, like all the loveliest flowers of the meadow, Hylas nursed on the nymphs' knees. There are, too, more homely figures like the fishermen who care only for their work and whose huts are full of tackle, the faithful dogs who bark at Heracles and make him compare them favourably with men, the pair of matrons who go with great bother and fuss to see a royal procession. There is the strange, moving figure of Simætha, who tries to bring back her unfaithful lover by magic, and when the winds and the sea are silent tells the tragic story of her love, calling on the moon to help her or to kill her lover if he remains untrue. All that matter here are the emotions, and even when they are painful or terrible, their force is mitigated by the silent sea, the blue sky, the climbing vines and the shady trees. There is always sweetness in this world of sun and song.

The Alexandrian poets, especially Callimachus and Theocritus, found many followers, and imitations of them helped poetry to survive, to maintain a consistent, if quiet, life. Though its scope was limited, it found a new source of vitality in the extension of Greek culture to the East and refreshed itself with an Oriental richness and intensity. The followers of Theocritus, Moschus (fl. 150 B.C.), Bion (fl. 120 B.C.) and the anonymous author of the *Lament for Bion* had none of their master's economy or restraint, but they had at least an exuberance which reveals itself in accumulated imagery and unrestrained emotions. Their verse has an authentic rhythm ; their pathos has a touch of rhetoric but is undeniably touching ; their refrains and repetitions give some of the force of a litany. Moschus has even picturesque qualities and something akin to poetic wit. Neither he nor Bion attempted to rival Theocritus, and their poetry is much more monotonous than his. But both in Bion's *Lament for Adonis* and in the *Lament for Bion* there is a sweet flow of lyrical melancholy, and though the thoughts may seem trite or strained, the lines are still melodious and compelling. The rich imagery is still chosen for its imaginative claims.

In the end, however, the revival of the epigram by Callimachus was to determine the future of Greek poetry. In the vast collection of the *Greek Anthology* the poetry of a thousand years is preserved, and it is remarkable how well the later products hold their own in the presence of the early. Though the verse becomes more elaborate and simplicity almost disappears, the many poets represented in this collection have often something to say, some moment of beauty or excitement worth recording. Even though they wrote by rule, carefully following the example of their predecessors, they have still their share of originality, giving an unfamiliar turn to a trite theme or adding a few words of just observation to redeem it from banality.

In the first days of its revival the epigram aimed almost at a Simonidean grace. Leonidas of Tarentum (fl. 274 B.C.) and Asclepiades (fl. 290 B.C.) were trained in a school which believed in restraint, and their delicate, tender poems, inspired by death or love or simple scenes of the country-side, have no trace of rhetoric. In a few lines they crystallize some moment which has stirred their imagination, and though it may be some very simple theme, like a wayside grave or a girl's book of poems or a lonely shepherd, their sincerity keeps it just as they felt it. Every word rings true, and though it would have been easy to add ornament and underline the effects, neither yields to the temptation. Even when Leonidas attempts on a larger scale the great theme of the passing of time and finds a truly noble imagery for his thought, he carefully eschews all the familiar exaggerations. Trained in the study of great masterpieces and humbled by the thought of their own inferiority, Leonidas and Asclepiades know at least where their gifts lie and strain from their sensitive experience a few moments of pure beauty.

In other hands the epigram found a greater fullness and perhaps a greater life. Meleager (fl. 90 B.C.) came from Gadara in Syria, and though he was no mean craftsman he brought into the elegiac an Oriental warmth and colour. His work is mainly concerned with love, but his attitude towards it owes little to tradition. For him passion was something violent and destructive, and his poems to Heliodora are written with the heat and concentration of a man who sacrifices everything to love and judges everything in relation to it. His original fancy finds symbols in the mosquito and the cicada; at the feast or in spring he is reminded of his love. His style is elaborate and highly coloured. He piles up his adjectives and uses recondite words. But he is always sure of his effect, and at times, when he mourns over Heliodora's death, he touches a truly tragic emotion. The fierce onset of grief breaks through his love of fine phrases and he writes in simple and touching words.

Apart from this tradition of poetry the later Hellenistic age was hostile to literature. Science pursued its course undaunted. The new philosophies of the Stoics, Cynics, and Epicureans, produced reams of treatises whose remains show few traces of style or imagination. It was not really till the Mediterranean world was absorbed into the Roman Empire that Greek literature found a new life. In that staid and ordered civilization Rome always looked to Greece as the mother of art and philosophy, and where there was such a demand, a supply inevitably followed. There was even something in the Roman conception of life which appealed to some thoughtful Greeks. In the ruin of their own world they found in Rome a substitute and a consolation, an ideal which stirred some innate austerity in them and redeemed the general sense of failure. The first signs of this impact may be seen in Polybius (c. 198–117 B.C.), who was inspired by the rise of the Roman Empire to write a history that is a worthy successor of the great work of Thucydides.

Polybius spent sixteen years as a hostage in Rome, became an intimate friend of Scipio Africanus, and developed a deep and detached appreciation of the Roman achievement. Though he seems never to have read Thucydides, he became his intellectual successor in his approach to history. His purpose was to tell of the advance of Roman power from the eve of the Second Punic War in 220 B.C. to the conquest of Macedonia in 168 B.C. He gives his reasons concisely : " Our own times have witnessed a miracle, and it consists in this. Fortune moved all the affairs of the world towards one quarter and constrained all things to tend to one and the same goal. And so it is the special note of my work to bring under one purview for my readers the means and the manipulations which fortune employed for this end." Like Thucydides he chose his subject well and wrote not for others' enjoyment, but for their instruction. He wanted his work to be useful to men of action who should profit by the lessons of the past. What makes him a good historian is his unremitting zeal for the truth. He was extremely critical in his use of evidence even when it came from unimpeachable sources. He insisted that the historian should have political experience and visit all the sites mentioned in his history. Though he seems to have had some metaphysical notion of the part played by fortune in human affairs and even to have accepted the Pythagorean and Platonic notion that history recurs in cycles, he remained remarkably detached, fair and scientific. He always displays his evidence and gives his reasons for his conclusions. If in consequence his work lacks the finish of Thucydides, it is of great interest as an exercise in historical method. Despite his workmanlike style and his admirable sense of arrangement, he has none of Thucydides' emotional and intellectual power. But he was a good historian, and in an age of rhetoricians and moralists, his work shines like a patch of light between clouds.

History, however, produced no more writers to equal Polybius, and when the triumph of Augustus stimulated a revival in Greek letters, the best minds turned to theoretical subjects. Greek literature had become part of Roman education and for the first time literary criticism became popular. Much of it is concerned with petty points of style and grammar, but in the treatise *On the Sublime* an anonymous author of the Augustan age has left the first known work which views poetry and prose from a purely æsthetic standpoint. His object is to analyse the Sublime, and he brings to his task an acute mind, a wide reading, and an impeccable taste. Quoting Moses and Sappho, illustrating his point by a contrast between Pindar and Bacchylides, he is always illuminating, and many of his judgments, such as his comparison of the *Iliad* with the *Odyssey* or his distinction between genius and talent, are in their way final. He is full of happy comparisons ; Demosthenes resembles a thunderbolt and Cicero a spreading fire. He has a happy knack of telling us why he enjoys a poem or in what its special greatness consists. He is full of good phrases ; the *Odyssey* is a " comedy of manners " and the adventures of Odysseus are " dreams of Zeus." His temper is admirably noble, and he is genuinely touching when he describes the literary barrenness of his own day and ascribes it to the prevailing desire for money.

But the best minds turned to more abstract subjects even than literature and found in philosophy a refuge from political tangles and a consolation for the political excitements from which they were excluded. In its simplest form this tradition was responsible for the best-known and most popular writer of the Græco-Roman world. Plutarch (A.D. 45–125) was a native of Bœotia, and though he had many chances of fame and wealth, he preferred to live quietly at home and write. His voluminous works fall into two sections, the *Morals* and the *Parallel Lives*. The *Morals* are a collection of eighty essays and their title gives little indication of their varied contents. Plutarch was a great reader. He liked elementary science and wrote on " The face in the moon " and " The sagacity of animals." A student of literature, he accused Herodotus of maliciously distorting facts, or

compared Aristophanes with Menander. Interested in all questions of religion, he writes
on the Pythian Oracle or tells the story of
how a voice was heard from the island of
Paxos saying " When you reach the Palodes,
tell them that great Pan is dead." But his
fundamental and abiding interest was in
ethics. He liked to write helpfully about envy
or gossip or false shame. He has always
something sensible to say and his advice,
though often homely, is usually good. Such,
indeed, are his nobility and humanity that
these tracts are never sermons. A man of
simple affections and strong domestic ties, he
writes sympathetically about married life
and the love of children without falling into
bathos or sentimentality.

He was also a great collector of peculiar
customs and beliefs, and in his *Table Talk*
an infinity of topics are discussed, from " Why
is A the first letter of the alphabet ? " to
" Do the Jews abstain from pork because they
worship pigs or because they detest them ? "
But the real wealth of his reading appears to
more useful advantage in the famous *Parallel
Lives*. In these forty-six biographies of Greek
and Roman statesmen grouped in pairs Plutarch has tapped many sources lost to us,
and the material collected is invaluable. But
as literature they are full of charm. Plutarch's
love of anecdotes and moralizing is limited
by his admirable eye for a good story. He
knew how to delineate personality, especially

that of men in action and defeat. The words he puts on his subjects' lips are indeed his own, redolent of his patient, enduring soul, but they are often magnificent. Shakespeare read him in North's translation, and some of the most famous words in his Roman plays are close verbal adaptations from Plutarch, and indeed the sustained tone of these plays, their restrained and noble manhood, owes much to the retired philosopher of Chæronea who pondered long on the difficulties and duties of man.

Philosophy makes its appeal in strangely different ways, and in the second century A.D. it was responsible for two widely divergent characters. The first was the lonely Roman emperor, Marcus Aurelius Antoninus (A.D. 121–180). His book of *Meditations*, written in an awkward and compressed Greek, is one of the most intimate documents of antiquity. In it this man of action, forced always to assume responsibility and to take great decisions, revealed his distaste for his position and recorded his efforts to find peace of soul during arduous campaigns on the Danube. He was a good Stoic who tried to identify himself with the " natural unity " of God, nature and man. This identification meant the complete suppression of personality and passion. Contemptuous alike of death and pain and glory, regarding pleasure as the sensation of beasts and immortality as an illusion, he had even to control his love of solitude as

a " mark of the most common sort of men,"
and to subordinate a natural melancholy to a
cheerful temper. Though he asked " What
more dost thou want when thou hast done a
man a service ? ", he seems too inhuman, too
detached. These confidences of a great soldier
leave out too much of his actual busy life.
But at times Marcus Aurelius has the grandeur
of Plato's philosopher-kings. His absence of
self-pity, his hardness on himself, his contempt
for the glories and miseries of his position,
have something indisputably grand in them.
If a man must annihilate himself, let him do
it in this way. At heart Marcus Aurelius
was a saint, longing for some self-transcen-
dence and absorption into the divine existence.
He looked always for the eternal reality, and
his words ring true when he says : " The
poet says, ' dear City of Cecrops.' Wilt thou
not say, ' dear city of God ' ? "

His contemporary, Lucian (A.D. 120–200),
showed to what different uses the philosophical tradition could be put. From it Lucian
inherited the form of the Platonic dialogue
and the vast material of philosophical thought,
but he used both for his own satirical purpose. He had absorbed all the culture of his
age ; he was a good poet ; he wrote in a
delightfully free and easy style. But he
found his chief satisfaction in mockery. He
was helped by a bright fancy, a gift for parody,
and a real sense of the ridiculous. He found
many targets for his wit. From the Olympian

gods he provided admirable comedy by emphasizing the absurd side of the legends and making his characters talk in quotations from the poets. In philosophers and philosophy he found no difficulty in exposing discords between theory and practice, and made fun of the dirtiness and ugliness of professional teachers. He found much to amuse him in the familiar figures of social life, and his ironical praise of the parasite's profession is admirably sustained. He parodied the writers of travels in his *True History*, which has much of the fancy and little of the bitterness of *Gulliver's Travels*. His wit was never too savage to be amusing, and he scores his best points by pretending to sympathize with his victims. He had, like other satirists, a sense of the futility of human life, and through his works runs the burden that man's activities are like bubbles in foam. But he was not merely a mocker. He had his gentle, even his sentimental, side. Some of his sketches of contemporary life show a real sympathy for the poor and unsuccessful; he uses his wit on their behalf and portrays their little ambitions with a charming understanding. Nor could he completely obliterate his poetic self. He wrote delicious vignettes that have more than a touch of Theocritean grace. He was an admirable critic of Greek art. He suffers, as satirists must, because he attacked institutions which have ceased to count, but he is always readable and usually amusing.

His jokes are still good; his touch is still light, his fancy undimmed by time.

In spite of such ribaldry the Platonic philosophy and Platonic temper still found adherents in some rare, gifted souls. The Neo-Platonists treated the *Dialogues* as sacred books and based on them a Platonism which the founder would hardly have recognized. Most of their work lies outside our present scope, but Plotinus (A.D. 204–270) cannot be left unmentioned. His whole life was devoted to the effort to give back the Divine in himself to the Divine which is the All. His *Enneads* were edited posthumously from his lectures, and lack both shape and clarity. Their power lies in the mystical vision which pervades them. Plotinus may write in the style of Aristotle, but he has more than Plato's mystical exaltation. He aimed at a state where the self should be identified with the Whole, and though his language and his goal are religious, the means of salvation which he taught lay entirely through thought and knowledge. He turned his saintly temperament to the laborious analysis of reality, and though his argument is often difficult and his manner strictly intellectual, his work is illuminated by his sense of a permanent reality above fleeting things. To the discussion and description of this he brought an acuteness and brilliance which succeed just at those points where Plato fails. He can write with perfect confidence and tact of those mystical experi-

ences which were for him the justification
and goal of life. He describes the unearthly
quiet when the universal soul floods the world
" as the bright beams of the sun enlighten a
dark cloud and give it a golden border," or
the bliss which the individual souls find in
the One : " a pleasant life is theirs there ;
they have the Truth for mother, nurse, real
being, and nutriment ; they see all things,
not the things which are born and die, but
those which have real being ; and they see
themselves in others." He writes nobly of
that beauty which induces " wonderment,
and a delicious trouble, longing and love and
a trembling which is all delight." His wide
charity and nobility of soul are in notable
contrast to Plato's terror and lack of confidence, and though the ideal reality of which
he wrote lies outside ordinary comprehension,
he gives it at least a radiance and exaltation
which make it a real experience for others.

Such raptures were not, however, for the
mass of men, and the popular reading of the
third century A.D. was not philosophy but
romance. When Philostratus (A.D. 170–250)
wrote his *Life of Apollonius of Tyana*, he was
supposed to be writing the gospel of a divine
being whose shrine was set by the Empress
Julia Domna by those of Abraham, Alexander
and Christ. In his book there is much dull
moralizing, but such life as it has is derived
from the ancient tradition of popular story-
telling. Philostratus took his hero to the

East, where he performed some neat miracles and witnessed many interesting things from levitation to the catching of dragons with runes. His *Life* is a romance such as the age liked, and several novels survive to show how popular stories of adventure were. None of these can be compared with a good modern novel. They were written for uneducated people who were not interested in verisimilitude or characterization. They are full of brigands and miraculous escapes, of forced separations and unexpected meetings. Their plots are exceedingly complicated ; their style has few beauties. But once a fine poetical sense raised the Greek novel into something unusual and beautiful. Longus (A.D. c. 250) wrote his *Daphnis and Chloe* out of a genuine sensibility and love of nature. The story is of two children, brought up among the flocks and herds, who fall in love and after forced separation meet again. Its claim is its poetic quality. Longus writes with delicate insight of this life among natural things, and his characters have the simplicity of the animals among which they move. His pictorial eye creates many charming scenes, and he has quite a sense of psychology. His characters are much more than names. Even his style has merits. Its simplicity is perhaps affected and artificial, but it is well suited to this pastoral world where children of nature move against a delicate background of birds and beasts and flowers.

Meanwhile a slender stream of poetry pursued an even course. Under the Roman Empire there were many writers of good elegiacs, whose works survive in the great collection of the *Greek Anthology*. But one personality stands out for his idiosyncrasies and sincerity. Palladas (A.D. *c.* 360–*c.* 430) is neither a very skilful nor a very sympathetic writer. His poetry has some of the obviousness and metallic resonance of Latin verse, and he himself was an embittered, despairing and violent man. But his deadly earnestness tells. In all his epigrams there is hardly a word of hope or of goodwill. He saw that all was vanity, that man is born in tears and dies in tears, that all his speech is the prelude to an eternal silence. But the thought of this made him angry, and he lashed the world with blistering words. He had none of the old joy of paganism, none of the feeling that man must find what joy he can before the darkness closes round him. He preached against the flesh with the same fierce fanaticism that he turned against the Christian monks of the Thebaid. He belonged to a society which had lost its beliefs and especially its belief in itself, but his passion made him a poet, and his fierce, angry lines stand out in sharp relief against the milder and more decorous verse of his time.

In the fifth century A.D. the tradition of the epigram was supplemented by a curious revival of the epic. Quintus of Smyrna

239

(fl. A.D. 400) wrote his *Posthomerica* in fourteen books and intended to fill the gap between the *Iliad* and the *Odyssey*. Written in a staid imitation of Homer's style and careful to avoid anachronisms, this last relic of an immemorial tradition makes few attempts to be great. There is little passion or heroism, but Quintus has his happy moments of landscape and even of pathos. He knew the country-side and drew pretty similes from it. He had a feeling for the picturesque aspects in the old stories. But he was no genius. His poem is dull; his verse moves slowly, and he was unwise to pit his gifts against Homer's. More adventurous was the *Dionysiaca* of Nonnus (fl. A.D. 420) which told in forty-eight books of the exploits, usually amorous, of Dionysus. Despite its ingenuity and technical accomplishment, despite its Oriental colouring and lack of decorum, the *Dionysiaca* soon begins to pall. Every effect is strained; all distinction and variety are ruined by the ceaseless straining after effect. In its first few lines it seems to promise a brave new world of fancy, but the unwearying rhetoric soon dulls the sensibilities, and a fundamental emptiness is revealed.

There is more to be said for Musæus (fl. A.D. 550) and his epic idyll of *Hero and Leander*. This poem, which inspired Marlowe, has traces of passion and sensual joy. The story of the separated lovers, of Leander's last swim to his death in the Hellespont and

Hero's death over his dead body, was perhaps a better subject than Musæus deserved, but he gave it something strange and beautiful, a fierce grandeur and wild tenderness which put life into his mannered style and carry the poem rapidly to its end. But Musæus, like others among his contemporaries, looked back to an irrecoverable past. In the Eastern Mediterranean, as in Italy, imagination and thought were no longer contented with the memory of Hellenic civilization. The triumph of Christianity had turned attention to a new mythology and a new scale of values. The old gods were turned into devils, the old stories held up to fierce disapprobation. Such art as existed was subordinated to the service of the Church, and popular literature consisted of hymns and theological tracts. And yet even when Justinian reigned in theocratic splendour at Byzantium, the old traditions were not quite dead. Rufinus (fl. A.D. 550), Paul the Silentiary (fl. A.D. 563) and Agathias (c. A.D. 536–582) revived the epigram to a late autumnal glory. They had an intimacy and an honesty which they clothed in coloured words. In the narrow circle of their official lives they still found moments of passionate love which lifted them above convention and impelled them to individual utterance. But with them came the end. The new Christian literature of Byzantium owed something perhaps to Hellenic models, but it used the vernacular tongue and looked to ideals of power and salvation which belonged to a new world. Its spiritual needs could not be satisfied by the old imagery or the old words, and the long career of Greek literature came to a close.

CONCLUSION

BOTH in its poetry and its prose Greek
literature appeals to the imaginative reason.
For its full appreciation it demands both a
concentration of the intellect and a responsive
sensibility, nor may any of its great masters
be understood and enjoyed unless he is approached with the conviction that he has
something worth saying and that he knows
how to say it. For of no Greek writer is it
true that his intelligence is inferior to his
literary gifts or that his style reflects ideas
which are of no interest. To none need we
bring that indulgence which we bring to
certain great poets of the Renaissance or the
Romantic Revival, in whom a delightful sensibility is combined with an inferior intelligence.
The great writers of Greece were men who
thought well and hard, who reinforced their
imaginative equipment with the strength
which only a firm grip on reality can give.
In this combination of gifts lies their peculiar
and distinctive claim. In Homer and the
tragedians, in Thucydides and Plato, the combination is plain enough. But even in Pindar,
even in Demosthenes, much of the value of
their work comes from the fundamental brain-
work which has gone to its making. It is

this which imparts not only their seriousness and candour, but also their concentration and balance. It is, in fact, this which underlies all right conceptions of " classical " literature.

The word " classical " has in the course of centuries been much misused in the partisan issues of controversy. In particular it has been used as the contrary of " romantic " to indicate those types of literature in which form has been considered more important than content. For such a use there is no justification in reality. In hardly any Greek writing, certainly in no great Greek writing, is content sacrificed to form. On the contrary, a meticulous seeker for perfection might find that some of Sophocles' plays are imperfectly constructed and that there are long irrelevances in some of the most famous dialogues of Plato. It would be easier to maintain that the Greeks were so interested in their matter that they were not always worried enough about its form, that they accepted the traditional limitations of their art without accommodating their themes properly to it. The difficulties which critics have found in Homer and Euripides are largely explicable on the notion that somewhat loose ideas of construction have been misunderstood in ages trained to sterner standards. Only perhaps in the greatest masterpieces like *King Œdipus* or the *Phœdo* can the strict advocate of classicism find the models he desires.

There is, however, another sense in which

Greek literature is essentially classical. Its writers have always a strong grip on reality. This may be seen not merely in the absence of the precious and esoteric, of all the lesser romantic qualities which make the " literature of escape," but more noticeably in the way in which all the writers are concerned with presenting something they think to be real. This is, of course, plainest in the lyric poets and historians, but it is equally fundamental in Homer and the tragedians. The world which Homer creates is four-square and solid. Its characters are like human beings, its landscape the recognizable landscape of Ægean lands. The great figures of Æschylus and Sophocles are moved by familiar emotions and stirred to act by motives which all men share. Even Euripides, who was interested in uncommon things and hampered by the traditions of tragedy, makes his men and women peculiarly intimate and alive. The fact is that much of the strength of Greek literature depends on its realism—not realism in the vulgar sense of stressing the ugly and familiar side of things, but in its true sense of creating something recognizably rooted in life.

At the back of Greek prose and poetry lies a genuine understanding of human nature, especially of its more permanent elements. Even a mystic like Plato conducts his revelations through characters not ultimately unlike ourselves, and the soaring flight of Pindar is inspired by the pride and pleasure of living men. The Greeks had always in their minds a conviction that literature was concerned with men and drew on human nature for its subject. Even when they passed beyond the visible everyday world into the garden of the Hesperides or the silent converse of the soul with itself, they were unable to shed their human attachments. They described their raptures in all too visible images and made their appeal to an ordinary desire for supramundane splendour. No doubt this essential humanism had its disadvantages. There is nothing in Greek literature resembling the abstract beauties of Dante's *Paradiso* or even the intellectual symbolism of the Second Part of *Faust*. Because too the Greeks were concerned with the permanent elements in man, there is no literature of the abnormal and strange. The wildest adventure of Euripides' curiosity never made him probe such obscure corners of the soul as Shakespeare probed in *Timon of Athens*. Still less could they leave humanity behind and move among disembodied allegories as Spenser did in the *Faerie Queene*. For better and for worse human nature determined both their choice and their treatment of subjects. Even the detached Thucydides has been accused by the advocates of economic history of attaching too much importance to personalities.

If Hebrew literature ultimately refers its standards to God, Greek refers to man.

Man provided the starting-point for every form of Greek writing, just as the human body provided the main subject for Greek sculpture. All that belonged to man might not find its way into literature, but without him it was inconceivable. The Greeks were the founders of humanism because their chief interest lay in man. They rejected Protagoras' doctrine that "man is the measure of all things" because it was not sufficiently human, and deprived man of his most cherished belief, his confidence that he can find the truth. It was precisely because of their interest in human nature that they were so often and so deeply concerned with the gods. They saw humanity surrounded and controlled by obscure powers, and naturally they tried to formulate its relation to them. But when they tried to define the nature of these powers, they could only conclude that they were like men but free from death and responsibility. Even Plato's passionate theism failed to rob his deity of human emotions. Nor could the Greeks ever regard man as nothing in comparison with the gods. They knew that he came from nothing and went to nothing ; they were often overwhelmed with the vanity of things ; but they never consoled themselves with the thought that man's insignificance was the measure of God's greatness. If the world was after all a futile illusion, the gods, no less than men, were figures in the shadow-show.

This interest and absorption in human

nature might in lesser hands have produced banal results. Innumerable dramatists and novelists have concerned themselves entirely with the ways of humanity, and their work has none the less passed into oblivion. The Greeks were saved partly by their inexplicable capacity for seeing life with the heightened powers of the imagination, partly by their strong intelligence which refused to be duped by sentiment or falseness. The first simplified experience for them and made it possible for them to express their visions in severe inherited forms. The second secured that every word was related to reality, that every touch convinced its audience that so, and not otherwise, must it have happened. Whatever came to them in their most exalted moments was submitted to a strict intellectual discipline before it passed into art, and not the least element in any creative work was the unremitting effort to understand and co-ordinate the mixed gifts of the imagination. The process which transformed the vast visions of Æschylus into the *Oresteia* must have been determined throughout by a strict desire to tell the truth and to display it through characters who were recognizably human.

Greek literature arose in a singularly homogeneous society, and the Greek writers addressed an almost common consciousness. If this limited the range of their topics and ideas, it added enormously to their power. They need waste no time in explanation ;

they need not trouble to prepare their audiences for novelties and paradoxes. They could assume a whole system of values, and their work has that fullness which can only come when the writer is one with his age, when he can work securely on an accepted scheme of things and form new shapes out of it. Just as Dante owes half his power to the mediæval culture which colours his work, so the Greek writers owe the steadiness of their outlook to a civilization which made them what they were and with which they were essentially one.

So in the end the greatness of Greek literature is that of Greek civilization. In this literature, more than in the remains of Greek sculpture and painting, we are brought into intimate contact with those men whom the Greeks honoured as inspired interpreters and the embodiment of all that was best in themselves. On it their appeal to posterity lies, and through it their achievement is revealed in its unique magnificence. In its insight and directness, in its unfailing sense of the real values of life and in its candid search for them, Greek literature has passed into the spiritual life of the world. But it has more sacred and more potent claims than this. It has that unfaltering style, shaped by the secret discipline of a landscape where all is clear outline and brilliant light; it has that power of concentrating on the object of its passionate thought until that object comes to life and exists of its own right; it has its own majestic harmonies of speech where words are perpetually reshaped into new patterns of enchantment. The spirit that breathes through these works is that of a people who believed in the dignity of man and displayed its belief in every word it wrote. It is their literature which keeps the Greeks alive. To it they confided their pride and their melancholy, their joy and their occasional self-abasement. Their words are still young, their thoughts still powerful. How did they do it? We do not know. They were the Greeks.

BIBLIOGRAPHY

GENERAL

GILBERT MURRAY: *Ancient Greek Literature.*
J. A. SYMONDS: *The Greek Poets.*
R. W. LIVINGSTONE: *The Greek Genius and its Meaning to us.*
F. R. EARP: *The Way of the Greeks.*
W. JAEGER: *Paideia.*

CHAPTER I

A. LANG: *The World of Homer.*
GILBERT MURRAY: *The Rise of the Greek Epic.*
C. M. BOWRA: *Tradition and Design in the Iliad.*
J. A. SCOTT: *The Unity of Homer.*
M. P. NILSSON: *Homer and Mycenae.*
W. LEAF: *Homer and History.*
W. J. WOODHOUSE: *The Composition of Homer's Odyssey.*
A. R. BURN: *The World of Hesiod.*

CHAPTER II

C. M. BOWRA: *Greek Lyric Poetry.*
U. VON WILAMOWITZ-MOELLENDORFF: *Sappho und Simonides.*
    Pindaros.
A. HAUVETTE: *Archiloque: Sa Vie et ses Œuvres.*

CHAPTER III

F. NIETZSCHE: *The Birth of Tragedy.*
A. W. PICKARD-CAMBRIDGE: *Dithyramb, Tragedy and Comedy.*
H. D. F. KITTO: *Greek Tragedy.*
GILBERT MURRAY: *Æschylus.*
T. B. L. WEBSTER: *Sophocles.*
C. M. BOWRA: *Sophoclean Tragedy.*
GILBERT MURRAY: *Euripides and his Age.*

BIBLIOGRAPHY

CHAPTER IV

J. B. Bury: *The Ancient Greek Historians*.
J. E. Powell: *The History of Herodotus*.
A. Hauvette: *Hérodote*.
F. M. Cornford: *Thucydides Mythistoricus*.
C. N. Cochrane: *Thucydides and the Science of History*.
J. H. Finley: *Thucydides*.

CHAPTER V

A. Couat: *Aristophane*.
Gilbert Murray: *Aristophanes*.
G. Norwood: *Greek Comedy*.

CHAPTER VI

A. E. Taylor: *Plato*.
J. Burnet: *Greek Philosophy, Thales to Plato*.
G. C. Field: *Plato and his Contemporaries*.
U. von Wilamowitz-Moellendorff: *Platon*.
S. H. Butcher: *The Poetics of Aristotle*.
I. Bywater: *Aristotle and the Art of Poetry*.
E. E. Sikes: *Greek Literary Criticism*.

CHAPTER VII

J. F. Dobson: *The Greek Orators*.
R. C. Jebb: *The Greek Orators*.
F. Blass: *Die attische Beredsamkeit*.
W. Jaeger: *Demosthenes*.
A. W. Pickard-Cambridge: *Demosthenes*.

CHAPTER VIII

U. von Wilamowitz-Moellendorff: *Hellenistische Dichtung*.
A. Couat: *Alexandrian Poetry*.
E. Cahen: *Callimaque et son Œuvre poétique*.
J. W. Mackail: *Select Epigrams from the Greek Anthology*.
F. A. Wright: *A History of Later Greek Literature*.

INDEX

INDEX

INDEX

GALAXY BOOKS FOR THE DISCRIMINATING READER